Making Critical Decisions

Readers are invited to view and download
the supplementary **Adaptable Matrix Template**
that accompanies *Making Critical Decisions*.

If you would like to download a free electronic copy of the
Adaptable Matrix Template, please visit
www.wiley.com/college/Snow

JB JOSSEY-BASS

Making Critical Decisions

A Practical Guide for Nonprofit Organizations

ROBERTA M. SNOW AND
PAUL H. PHILLIPS

Features an Easy-to-Use Matrix for Effective Decision Making

John Wiley & Sons, Inc.

Published by Jossey-Bass
A Wiley Imprint
989 Market Street, San Francisco, CA 94103-1741 www.josseybass.com

Wiley Bicentennial logo: Richard J. Pacifico

Jossey-Bass books and products are available through most bookstores. To contact Jossey-Bass directly call our Customer Care Department within the U.S. at 800-956-7739, outside the U.S. at 317-572-3986, or fax 317-572-4002.

Jossey-Bass also publishes its books in a variety of electronic formats. Some content that appears in print may not be available in electronic books.

Library of Congress Cataloging-in-Publication Data

Snow, Roberta.
    Making critical decisions: a practical guide for nonprofit organizations / Roberta M. Snow and Paul H. Phillips.—1st ed.
        p. cm.
    Includes bibliographical references and index.
        ISBN-13: 978-0-7879-7636-1 (cloth)
    1. Decision making. 2. Nonprofit organizations—Management. I. Phillips, Paul H. II. Title.
        HD30.23.S668 2008
        658.4'03–dc22

                                                                                2007028791

Printed in the United States of America

FIRST EDITION

HB Printing   10 9 8 7 6 5 4 3 2 1

CONTENTS

PART TWO

Making Critical Decisions

TABLES AND EXHIBITS

Tables

Exhibits

For
BOB

ACKNOWLEDGMENTS

WE ACKNOWLEDGE a number of individuals and institutions that helped us in the development of the project.

First and foremost, we thank Doug Bauer, who started us on this path, supported the development of the matrix, and through his review of an early version of the manuscript helped us produce a much more user-friendly book.

Others have played a variety of important roles at different stages of the project:

Linda Pickthorne-Fletcher, Paul Master-Karnik, Mark Weinstein, and Marc Scorca, who showed great patience in testing the prototype matrices.

Benna Wilde and the members of the Donors Forum of Chicago, who reviewed and commented on applications of the due diligence approach to charitable giving.

Christine James-Brown and Mary Strasser, who applied the approach to funding innovation at the United Way of Southeastern Pennsylvania.

The students who took part in the first decision-making workshop given through the University of Pennsylvania's Nonprofit Management and Leadership Program in the College of General Studies: Shawn Benjamin, Cheryl Diehl, Maureen Donovan, Marion Dorrah, Dona File, Joe Hartnett, Richard Hirsh, Sarah Janicki, Linda Mitchell, Ron Opher, Patrick Temple-West, Sofia Wynnytsky, and Laurie Zierer. All thoughtful professionals working with nonprofits, their practical comments were extremely useful in developing our final draft.

The Delaware Valley Society of Association Executives, in particular, Mike Taylor, Larry Caniglia, and Beth Goldstein, who gave us the opportunity to develop a training session for their membership based on the matrix approach and gather additional valuable feedback.

Colleagues at the West Chester University School of Business and Public Affairs: Dean Christopher Fiorentino, who generously supported the research and writing of the book; Charles McGee, chair of the Management Department, who encouraged and endorsed the project; and Evan Leach, who over the years has been a great academic partner and friend.

Colleagues at the University of Pennsylvania: Rosalie Guzofsky, who understands the importance of working across sectors and disciplines, and Tom McKenna, who reviewed the first draft of the manuscript from his perspective as both a teacher and nonprofit leader and provided us with constructive and detailed criticism.

Friend and colleague Stephen Broyles, whose keen editorial and common sense helped to make the final draft of the manuscript much more readable.

And, last but not least, the Jossey-Bass Nonprofit Leadership Series editors, who have shepherded the manuscript through development: Allison Brunner, who first laid eyes on it; Johanna Vondeling, who first shaped it; Dorothy Hearst, who guided the first draft or "mind dump"; and Jesse Wiley, who then brought the whole thing to completion with thoughtfulness and a great sense of humor.

THE AUTHORS

ROBERTA M. SNOW is a professor of management at West Chester University of Pennsylvania. Over the past two decades she has also held several positions at the University of Pennsylvania, most recently as director of Nonprofit Management and Leadership Programs. Prior to that appointment, she was the director of the Wharton Cultural Management Project and a faculty member affiliated with the departments of Management and Public Policy at the Wharton School, where she taught graduate classes in nonprofit administration related to cultural institutions.

Snow holds a Ph.D. in social systems sciences from the University of Pennsylvania's Wharton School and has focused much of her academic and consulting work on the appropriate application of strategic and operational planning methods developed in the commercial sector to nonprofit and government organizations. She is the author of several books and numerous articles on planning and organization change and sits on the editorial board of several management publications.

In recent years, she has worked with numerous nonprofit organizations on planning and management issues including Rockefeller Philanthropy Advisors, the Robert Wood Johnson Foundation, Rebuilding Together, the Pennsylvania Horticultural Society, the Center for Research Integrity at Children's Hospital of Philadelphia, the United Way of Southeastern Pennsylvania, OperaAmerica, the Institute of Contemporary Art, the Devereux Foundation, the Kennedy Center for the Performing Arts, and the National Endowment for the Arts.

PAUL H. PHILLIPS is a consultant who has worked with a variety of clients, with primary concentration in nonprofit organizations and manufacturing companies, working to improve the efficiency of their infrastructures and developing methodologies to optimize operating assets. He has also worked extensively with venture capital groups in building investment relationships with growing companies.

Upon graduating from the University of Minnesota, Phillips began his career as a certified public accountant with KPMG, where he ultimately became a partner. During his tenure there, his clients included predominantly developmental-stage enterprises and other rapidly growing companies, as well as nonprofit organizations. In addition to audit-related responsibilities, his work emphasized providing assistance in the development of strategic plans and modeling their economic viability.

A lifelong endurance athlete, Phillips is the past president of the Team Birke Ski Education Foundation, which raises money and provides coaching for talented Nordic skiers in preparation for international and Olympic competition.

You're moving into a land of both shadow and substance,
of things and ideas. You've just crossed over into the
Twilight Zone!

—*Rod Serling*

WE HAVE SPENT our professional lives working in what often seems like the twilight zone. Half of our time has been spent with commercial enterprises—for-profit businesses. The other half has been devoted to nonprofit organizations. Our experiences in both worlds have blurred together and led us to believe that the two sectors can learn much of substance from each other. Ideas, tools, and techniques can be adapted and transferred from one to the other. This book is about one of those tools: the decision matrix.

Most of our work studying and consulting to nonprofits has focused on the development of strategies that bring about positive and sustainable change, and much of that work seeks to help groups through the strategic

1

planning process. Although developing workable strategies is a complex and sometimes lengthy process, most nonprofit managers have a good understanding of what it takes to plan for their organizations. Then several years ago, our work took a slightly different turn when we began to get requests to help with specific problems or situations that emerged outside the normal planning process. You could call these strategic surprises.

You have probably faced similar situations or at least know of organizations that have had similar experiences. Among our more memorable engagements are these:

- Helping an organization that had always struggled to balance its budget allocate an unexpected and unrestricted major windfall bequest

- Designing philanthropic funds to support innovation with the greatest likelihood of success

- Developing a comprehensive formal decision support system for an organization that had previously relied on informal feedback

- Guiding a group through an extensive and painful retrenchment process after a significant and unanticipated cut in funding

In every one of these situations, the organizations were dealing with something new. Boards and managers faced significant and complex problems or opportunities and were uncertain of their options. In other words, we were called to come in when the leadership didn't know exactly what to do and couldn't sleep at night. They had entered their own managerial twilight zone.

This book grew out of those experiences. Whenever we were hired to deal with a strategic surprise, we found ourselves digging into our commercial bag of tricks. When the organization faced an opportunity, we asked, "How can the organization do the most with the resources it has at its disposal?" When we were looking at a problem, we asked, "How can the organization best cut its losses and position itself for the future?" We realized we were thinking like investors and that what was standard and effective practice in the investment community could be very helpful to our nonprofit clients.

Based on our knowledge of both sectors, we developed this book as a guide for nonprofits facing novel and critical situations. It is based on two methods widely used in the investment community that we use with our clients: the due diligence process and the decision matrix.

We use the term *due diligence* as investors do. It's the detailed and structured process they use to thoroughly examine and assess their options for committing funds. The similarities between investors and nonprofit managers who are making hard choices are striking. Both groups have limited time and resources, and both desire to bring about the best outcome with the least risk. Adapting investor due diligence to the nonprofit context gives us a way to approach critical decisions.

Our decision matrix is based on this process. It is a graphic way to capture all the key issues as well as the opinions of those involved in helping to make the decision. This type of tool is nothing new. Managers use it to capture data to support decision making all the time. We have simply taken the matrices that investors use to support their due diligence and tailored it to the needs of nonprofits.

We have used this modified due diligence approach along with the matrix with numerous nonprofits over the past decade, and they are useful and work. We believe they are successful methods that most managers will find helpful and can easily add to their repertoire. And that's why we wrote this book.

The chapters in Part One provide an overview of decision making and the due diligence process. Chapter One contains a general review of successful decision-making strategies that nonprofits already use. There are three areas in which managers have successful ways of making choices: habitual, recipe, and planning decisions. Habitual decisions are based on what the decision maker has informally learned through experience: he or she knows what works and what doesn't and incorporates this understanding into daily routine decision making. Recipe decisions are based on rules and standard practices. And planning decisions are based on detailed analysis, discussion, and trade-offs decision makers use within their regular strategy, operations, and budgeting processes. We then discuss the decisions that force decision makers out of their comfort zones and discuss what sets these critical choices apart from the others. They pose new situations, capture the element of strategic surprise, expose the organization to considerable risk or have the potential to result in substantial reward, require a significant commitment of resources, or compel quick action.

Chapter Two outlines the commercial due diligence process and how it can be used to support making hard choices in nonprofits. Specifically, we discuss three guiding principles: minimize risk, maximize leverage, and ensure sustainability. We detail how investors screen for risk and examine the processes that can be put in place to help manage it. By *leverage,* we mean the return on investment. Ideally the organization gets more out than it puts in, and this chapter discusses how this can also be measured in terms of non-profit impact. Finally, we explain what is needed to sustain the impact and guarantee future stability.

Chapter Three details the specifics of who does what and how within due diligence. These include types of critical decisions as well as phasing (or staging) the decision to reduce risk. We discuss three group roles critical to the decision process: the primary decision makers—those lucky individuals who have the ultimate authority and responsibility for the decision; individuals who have specialized knowledge that inform the decision; and those who have to be informed of the final choice and why it was made. We also break down the decision into three possible types. First, there are binary decisions: do something or nothing. Second, there are decisions among dissimilar options, where you have to find some way to make comparisons between things that on the surface seem to vary so widely that there doesn't immediately seem to be a basis for comparison. And, third, we address decisions among similar options, where the differences in the details become key to making the best choice. Finally, in this chapter, we look at how to stage the decision to minimize risk. After you know who will be playing what role and what type of options you are dealing with, you determine where you are in the life cycle of the new idea.

We divide any change imposed on the organization into four phases: feasibility, pilot, implementation, and cutback. The feasibility stage deals with exploring the concept to see if it makes sense before committing resources and taking action. The pilot allows testing the new idea in a limited way to see if it actually works in practice. If the pilot is successful, the organization can move to a full commitment of resources and implement the decision completely. Finally, there are those times when an idea, practice, program, or system is obsolete. This is the cutback stage, where decision makers decide if they should stop doing something they've been doing and reallocate the resources that have been used to support it.

The final chapter in Part One, Chapter Four, pulls all these elements together with the introduction to the matrix tool. The matrix is presented as a simple grid, with the due diligence criteria listed down the left side. These criteria are weighted using a system that reflects their importance to the organization making the choice. The decision makers are listed across the top. They score each of the due diligence criteria, reflecting their opinions about how closely an option meets those criteria. The boxes within the grid are used to record each person's score about each item. We discuss how the tool can be used to record and present data, enhancing communication and accountability.

The chapters in Part Two provide a step-by-step guide to using the matrix tool in successive stages of due diligence: feasibility, pilot, implementation, and cutback. These stages are addressed in Chapters Five through Eight. Each of these chapters is written as a how-to handbook, helping you assemble your decision by leading you through the relevant due diligence questions one by one. Each of these chapters includes illustrative minicases based on some of our actual experiences showing how the matrix can be adapted and the results formatted in a range of different situations.

Chapter Nine looks at how different groups working in nonprofits—boards, executive directors, managers, funders, and consultants—can use the method set out in Chapters Five through Eight. Each group plays a different role in gathering information, facilitating the process, and communicating the results, and it is helpful to see how this approach can be used to help them do their particular jobs.

Finally, Chapter Ten brings us full circle. It provides a checklist that summarizes the book's contents. And it does so in a way that allows you to retrace your steps through the due diligence process. So when you do have a strategic surprise, you can go back, use the checklist as a quick and easy reference, evaluate the decision at hand, and approach it with the due diligence it merits. **And for those readers who want to develop their decision-making skills further, the Appendix provides an example of how a simplified version of the matrix tool can be used.**

So if you too occasionally find yourself in the managerial twilight zone, read on.

PART 1

About Decision Making

1

The Art and Science of Decision Making

PUTTING THEORY INTO PRACTICE

Nothing is as practical as a good theory.
—Kurt Lewin

An ounce of action is worth a ton of theory.
—Friedrich Engels

NONPROFIT LEADERS AND MANAGERS ARE, for the most part, very good at making decisions. If they weren't, their organizations wouldn't function. It is our goal to help them make even better ones. With a clear idea of the theory, they can begin to understand what already works and where nonprofits can improve.

Decision theory is extremely practical, but the really good stuff tends to be formal, with lots of exciting mathematics to plow through.[1] Because we would like this book to be read and used to actually make better choices, our first goal is to distill the relevant theory to make it as painless, accessible, and useful as possible.

The first part of this chapter is devoted to discussing what works and providing enough theory to explain why. It next looks at the decisions that pose problems for even the most experienced executives. With this overview, we then develop a set of workable guidelines for addressing difficult decisions supported by theory and grounded in practice.

What Works

Successful nonprofit leaders have a limited range of decisions they deal with on a routine basis. Specifically, three types of decisions represent the majority of choices they make:

- Habitual decisions

- Recipe decisions

- Planning decisions

Although the range is small, each of these categories includes a number of familiar decisions that make up a large portion of management activity.

Habitual Decisions

> *Curious things habits. People themselves never knew they had them.*
>
> —*Agatha Christie*

Our lives progress through a series of decisions. Everyday experience demonstrates this. If you try to capture every detail of every choice you make from the time you get up in the morning until the time you go to bed at night, you will immediately find yourself on the road to insanity. Which side of the bed to get up on? Left or right foot on the floor first? Yes or no to slippers? Run or walk to the bathroom? (For the sake of modesty, we will omit the detailed bathroom choices. Use your imagination here.) Breakfast this morning, yes or no? If yes, hot or cold cereal? Which kind of juice? Coffee or tea? Caffeinated or decaf? And so on. Even entertaining this type of chronicling quickly leads to the realization that we are constantly making choices, and we make them without thinking, as if on decision-making autopilot.

We build our individual routines, our collection of everyday habits, over a lifetime, learning from a process of trial and error. The technical term for this way of learning what works and doesn't work and putting that knowledge into practice is called a *heuristic*. Most of us have a repertoire of heuristics for every facet of our lives, including the decisions we make in our work.[2]

As a result, most individual decisions made in nonprofits are informal and based on learning from success and failure in similar situations. For example, how individuals organize their work space, behave in groups, and communicate with external constituents are all conditioned by prior experience. This is true no matter how large or small the organization might be. Effective executives, board members, employees, and volunteers are often characterized as "knowing their stuff." They habitually make good decisions, and they seem to do it artfully, with ease and confidence. This is a tribute to how they have learned from experience and how this individual knowledge translates into action.

Recipe Decisions

> *Most managers were trained to be the thing they most despise—bureaucrats.*
>
> *—Alvin Toffler*

Heuristics will get you only so far in terms of management effectiveness. Once individuals become part of organizations, their decisions become constrained and shaped by various sets of rules. In other words, the minute you cast your lot with a nonprofit, you become a bureaucrat. In spite of all the negative baggage associated with the term, bureaucracy is not necessarily a bad thing; in fact, it is a necessary thing. Rules provide needed structure and predictable processes in complex social groups. When work is divided up, as it must be in any organization, it is essential to have consistent systems to coordinate and monitor the various pieces. Otherwise the parts can diverge and undermine the organization as a whole. For example, without the discipline of the budgeting process, successful programs might grow too quickly and exhaust the organization's resource base. Bureaucracy is a practical administrative system that ideally supports effectiveness and should contribute to efficiency.[3]

Bureaucratic decisions follow recipes. They are prescribed by an existing set of explicit rules. You follow the rules, and the resulting process leads you to the correct action. Individuals have little or no discretion. It is indeed much like working from a cookbook; it's by-the-book decision making. There are only certain areas where strict *recipe* or bureaucratic decision making actually takes place in nonprofits.[4]

First, complying with the law usually involves a number of recipe decisions.[5] Most nonprofits routinely submit their required filings to the Internal Revenue Service and appropriate state regulatory bodies. They also operate according to their own incorporation documents and by-laws.

Second, many nonprofits conform to sets of standards imposed by expert external bodies and in so doing apply recipe decision making.[6] For example, large institutions such as universities and hospitals operate according to standards developed by national and regional accrediting bodies. And some nonprofit employees, such as social workers and physicians, adhere to professional standards of practice to maintain their licenses and certifications.

Finally, sets of best practices provide recipes or models for management decisions.[7] Successful organizations are studied, and the rules that guided their success are generalized for application by other groups. In essence, informal heuristics are formalized. In recent years, approaches such as the balanced scorecard[8] and 360-degree evaluation[9] have provided templates for strategic and human resource decisions. This is the organizational equivalent of swapping award-winning casserole recipes.

While most will agree that compliance, standards, and best practices are all good things, the mechanical nature of recipe decisions remains disturbing. It is only natural to fear bureaucracy run amok and working with soulless robot-like bureaucrats. Bureaucratic rules aim to make choices automatic, with little room for improvement. They cut off individuality, creativity, and responsibility. No matter how good an award-winning casserole is, it is human nature to fiddle with the recipe to make it better. Effective nonprofit leaders know when a recipe is needed, and if so, whether it should be followed to the letter or used as a general set of guidelines that can be adapted for their specific organization.

Planning Decisions

> *In preparing for battle, I have always found that plans are useless, but planning is indispensable.*
>
> —*Dwight D. Eisenhower*

There are times when heuristics and recipes, those off-the-shelf plans, don't work. When leaders are faced with new challenges for the future—the non-profit equivalent of doing battle—the process used in decision making is key, and it is fundamentally different from the first two processes we have discussed. When leaders make planning choices, the underlying method for making habitual and recipe decisions is turned inside out.

First, planning decisions don't rely on set behaviors or rules with the assumption that they will lead to the desired outcome. Instead, planning decisions begin with the desired future outcome or goal. These goals can be broad and strategic, such as, "Make programs available to all eligible individuals in our service area," or, "Establish an endowment." Or they can be more specific and operational: "Provide database training for all administrative staff," or, "Develop a comprehensive assessment process for the organization's current programs." What is to be done—the goal—drives how the decisions are made.

Second, because there is no right way to pursue the goal prescribed at the beginning, the planning process is messy. Deciding how to proceed often involves consultations with others who will be affected by the decision, discussions with external experts familiar with similar situations, a review of relevant documents and existing information, and the collection and analysis of new data. Once a leader has reached a decision, taking action depends on effectively building support for the change.

Shifting strategic direction, implementing a new program or terminating an existing one, or putting in place a new administrative system or process all reflect this type of complex decision making.

Unlike habitual decisions that shape routine work and recipe decisions that ensure performance in specific areas of nonprofit operations, planning decisions move the entire organization by fits and starts forward into the future. In other words, habitual and recipe decisions promote consistency and stability, while planning decisions support change and progress.[10]

What Doesn't Work

There cannot be a crisis this week. My schedule is already full.
—Henry Kissinger

When it's business as usual, well-developed habits, recipes, and planning are effective decision strategies. Unfortunately, we do not live in a world that is tranquil or even reasonably consistent from one week to the next. Situations continually arise when managers face new and challenging choices, and the tried-and-true ways of making decisions do not work well. In many cases, decisions have to be made and implemented quickly. When timely decisions are important for the future viability of the organization, management faces a crisis.

We think many of our readers would like to echo Dr. Kissinger's comment given the pressures on their own organizations. It rings true because current sector dynamics increase the likelihood that a crisis can emerge in any nonprofit organization at any time.

Today's world of nonprofits can be characterized in part by the following well-documented trends:

- Sustained and, in many cases, increased demand for services and programs
- Uncertain funding from government and private sources
- Increased costs of operation
- Increased competition with other nonprofits and, in some cases, commercial organizations
- Increased pressure for transparency and accountability

These dynamics create an environment that can spawn an organizational crisis at almost any time.[11]

Organizations are best equipped to handle crises when they occur during routine planning. For example, during the course of developing a strategic plan, management is already in the process of grappling with environmental challenges, and so if a new competitor emerges or a constituent group requests a significant change in programming, there are systems in place to handle it. Or if a major funder changes policy that will reduce an anticipated grant in the middle of annual budgeting, the necessary trade-offs can be made within the process. The crisis issue can be addressed by the appropriate stakeholders in already scheduled meetings. Options about how to proceed can be aligned with mission and other organizational goals and objectives, resources can be discussed and budgeted, and implementation can be coordinated with other activities.

Most crises, however, do not conveniently coincide with an organization's planning activities. They first emerge as issues for organizations in the course of routine work in a functional area. For example, nonprofits become aware of major funding opportunities, changes in grant-making policy, and donor initiatives in the day-to-day work of their development or advancement departments. Because of the potential impact of any of these on the organization's programmatic and organizational stability and overall financial health, the development staff must inform the right management and staff groups so that the potential impact of the decisions can be assessed and the appropriate funding mix pursued.

There are also times when crisis situations emerge by accident, sometimes outside work hours. For example, during a casual conversation at dinner, an executive director learns that a building that seems perfectly suited for her organization's current and future planned programming has just become available. A capital project might not have been part of the organization's plans, but the potential opportunity of a new space sets a critical decision in motion.

These are the situations that keep nonprofit leaders up at night. Some managers cope with the stress by subscribing to the notion, "Don't sweat the small stuff—and it's all small stuff."[12] However, addressing this type of critical decision—nonroutine, complex, risky, and with major consequences—is important for any organization. How leadership individually or collectively learns how to sweat the big stuff and make the right choices is key to any nonprofit's future stability and vitality.

Reacting Versus Responding

> *We barely have time to react in this world,*
> *let alone rehearse.*
>
> *—Ani DiFranco*

Critical decisions are almost always accompanied by a sense of urgency. This is what makes them distinct from planning decisions. The importance of the decision and the limited time available to make and implement it create the crisis environment. If you ignore these decisions or take too long, you might miss a major opportunity or even court disaster and humiliation. These are the decisions that lead down the road to organizational glory or to ruin. In these situations, managers tend to react instead of respond, and it often seems they barely have time to do that.[13]

When you react to a situation, the emphasis is on the action, the goal, or the desired outcome, not the decision-making process that leads to the action. The assumption is that the more quickly you decide, the sooner action can be taken, and the sooner the crisis is resolved. You certainly don't have time to rehearse, and sometimes you have the feeling that you are improvising. In other words, you are making and implementing important decisions by the seat of your pants.

This style of decision making is deeply ingrained in modern management culture, regardless of the sector. We value leaders who can get things done, especially when tough choices have to be made. Action is concrete. It's evidence of progress. Reflection is not. Thinking about an issue can be equated with indecisiveness or doing nothing.[14]

Critical situations mesh well with a management culture that already values expedient decisions. However, a reactive approach can weaken an organization over time. In the rush to action, decision makers often suffer from managerial tunnel vision. They cut corners to get the job done fast. Sometimes they focus on short-term and limited results and ignore the possible long-term consequences and impact on other parts of the organization. They do not involve appropriate stakeholders or collect the right information. Time pressure can also result in amplified emotions that replace rational and objective analysis. Trade-offs and results are overly dependent on the gut instincts of the decision makers. Often such decisions are not part of established processes, and they are not recorded. Their impact on the organization and the community cannot be tracked, so there is no reliable way to learn from good and bad choices or to communicate them adequately.

Ad hoc approaches to major new decisions can create significant future problems for the organization. Most of these have to do with the lack of consistency and coordination in the decision-making process. These are:

- Mission creep
- Conflict
- Inefficiency
- Diminished accountability

Each of these deserves some attention, because an effective decision-making approach should address all of them.

Mission Creep

The decision may not support or fit the organization's overall mission or its shorter-term strategic goals. If decisions are not aligned with organizational strategies, they can cumulatively lead to mission creep, whereby the organization moves away from its central mission bit by bit. For example, over the past two decades, many performing arts organizations have developed education departments in response to funder demands. They have accordingly shifted, some more successfully than others, from the business of performing to the business of education. In some cases, they have changed their resource mix, strained relationships with dedicated arts education organizations, and been challenged by school districts and teachers' unions.

As a result, these organizations have had to develop the capacity not only to support ongoing programming but also to manage a new set of external relationships.

Conflict

An organization that does not involve the appropriate individuals or groups in making critical decisions can end up working at cross purposes with itself. For example, staff members at a local community development agency that does neighborhood programming begin talks with a local school in the course of their routine work. They develop a partnership without realizing that their organization's education department already has a plan for developing more expansive programming across the entire school district. This creates a set of awkward relationships internally and with an important external stakeholder group.

Inefficiency

An organization working without appropriate staff involvement can have difficulty identifying and using the existing organizational expertise and resources to appropriately inform and implement the decision. Sometimes external expertise is sought when it is actually resident and untapped in the organization. This happens frequently with technology decisions. For example, one department might choose to purchase database software when the organization already owns and uses a similar system in another department. Effort is duplicated and unnecessary expense incurred.

Diminished Accountability

Perhaps the most important consequence of handling important decisions in a reactive manner is that responsibility for the decision and accountability for its impact become diluted. For example, a development department staff member might decide to pursue a foundation initiative without adequately consulting the appropriate groups in order to make the grant deadline. The development staff member is not in a position to assume responsibility for the programmatic and financial impact of that decision.

Responding Versus Reacting

> *I shall keep you, and in responding to my passions yer*
> *hatred will kindle into love.*
>
> —*John Wayne, as Genghis Khan in* **The Conqueror,** *to*
> *Susan Hayward as the wild and untamed princess Bortai*

When decision makers respond, rather than just react, to a major opportunity or problem, they take the time to address the situation completely and carefully and then proceed thoughtfully and deliberately. They consult the right people and collect and assess the right information. They weigh the possible risks and rewards. And they develop an understanding of how implementing the decision will affect the organization as well as the broader community. In responding, they learn more about what is possible and can sometimes transform a problem into an opportunity. When the decision is made, it is truly an informed choice.

Because of the sense of urgency that accompanies critical decisions, responding requires a process that is well organized and efficient. The rest of this book is devoted to developing a comprehensive and practical approach to making good choices in critical situations. It is based on what nonprofit managers already do well and incorporates the following elements:

- Knowledge and expertise that managers have developed through their individual experience

- Rules, guidelines, and best practices that can support the decision going forward

- The organization's strategic and operating plans and planning processes

This process also offers a structure that helps avoid major coordination problems:

- It maintains strategic focus, avoiding mission creep.

- It is inclusive of the appropriate stakeholders, avoiding conflict.

- It addresses the resources and expertise available, avoiding inefficiency.

- It provides a way of recording and communicating the decision,
  increasing instead of diminishing accountability.

In the subsequent chapters, we build on these basic guidelines to develop
our approach to making critical decisions effectively and consistently.

2

Borrowing from Business

DUE DILIGENCE IN DECISION MAKING

I not only use all the brains that I have,
but all that I can borrow.
—Woodrow Wilson

A **PRACTICAL APPROACH** to critical decisions should include what nonprofits are already doing well, taking advantage of individual experience and knowledge and incorporating existing standards and plans. The complementary method we propose gives nonprofits an expanded set of tools for dealing with novel, complex, and time-sensitive decisions. Because it's an approach that is already widely used, we can dispense with the theoretical discussion.

All organizational sectors—government, nonprofit, and business— continually learn and borrow ideas and methods from each other. Government has adopted the results-based management practices widely used in commercial businesses to become more effective.[1] Management guru Peter Drucker encouraged businesses to apply the techniques developed by nonprofits for motivating and retaining volunteers to the management of highly mobile knowledge workers.[2] And nonprofits with their limited budgets have been particularly adept at letting the other groups develop, test, and sort out the management methods and then selecting what works and modifying it for their own needs. For example, nonprofits have successfully used the techniques of zero-based budgeting, management by objectives, and quality assurance. Therefore, we propose that nonprofits borrow one more time from business in order to fill the gaps in their decision-making repertoire.

Specifically, we propose that nonprofits adopt a standard method that commercial investors use to address new business opportunities to guide critical decisions. The nonprofit sector already has experience in successfully borrowing ideas from the investment community. Funding organizations in particular have explored and incorporated methods that venture capitalists use because they specifically address the commitment of outside resources to new ideas. Just as investors invest in businesses, philanthropies invest in nonprofits. As a result, funders have developed, tested, and now use a range of venture philanthropy approaches to support their grant making and oversight.[3]

We specifically focus on the mechanics of what investors do when faced with novel proposals: the due diligence process.[4] As you will see in this and the following chapter, borrowing this method complements the approaches already used in nonprofit decision making and provides organizations with a practical framework for making critical choices.

What Investors Do

Never invest your money in anything that eats or needs repairing.

—*Billy Rose*

The role of the investment community can be viewed as developing effective and sustainable businesses. Similarly, the work of nonprofit leaders is to develop effective and sustainable organizations that achieve their missions. Whenever a nonprofit commits resources to a new idea, it is investing in organizational change and improvement. So nonprofits are clearly in a position to learn from commercial investment practices.

Typically investors evaluate and act on new opportunities so they can commit their resources where they will generate the greatest return. Three primary principles guide investors' decision making: minimize risk, maximize leverage, and ensure sustainability.

THE THREE GUIDING PRINCIPLES OF INVESTORS' DECISION MAKING

Minimize Risk

In commercial situations, investors assume a financial risk by putting up their funds: if they make a poor decision, they can incur a loss. The company in which the money is being invested assumes not only the financial burden of the investment but also the risks associated with how those funds are used. For example, if the investment supports the development of a new product, the risk is whether the product will succeed or fail in the marketplace. Therefore, processes are put in place to assess the potential risk for both investor and company before the investment decision is made.

Maximize Leverage

Investors seek the greatest return on their investment, assuming the company is able to add economic value to their funds. Leverage is the degree to which the return is greater than the investment. The greater the leverage is, the greater the return on investment will be. For example, an investment of $100 that has a return of $125 has greater leverage than an investment of $100 that returns $110.

Ensure Sustainability

Once resources are committed, investors assess what is necessary to maintain their impact. Any change or innovation must be sustainable if it is to succeed in the long term. Therefore, investors must consider the long-term consequences of their decision, including the company's future resource requirements, infrastructure needs, and market conditions.

Defining Due Diligence

*What we hope ever to do with ease we may learn
first to do with diligence.*

—Samuel Johnson

The decision process that investors use is focused on fully understanding the risk, leverage, and sustainability issues related to each funding opportunity, so they can make informed decisions before taking action. Instead of reacting to a new prospect, investors respond with a standard routine. Before making a decision, they go through a process of due diligence.

Due Diligence in the Investment Community

The term *due diligence* has become part of ordinary management language. Some would say it has even been elevated to the status of jargon. When we use it in our everyday dealings, we usually mean a careful examination and evaluation of a particular situation or idea. In the legal and commercial world, it is a precise technical term that has different meanings depending on the context. For example, it has different legal connotations for those working in criminal law than it does for those working on environmental regulation.[5] And in business development, it refers to different processes depending on whether you are dealing with mergers and acquisitions, partnerships, or investments.[6] We limit our discussion in this book to the due diligence process used in making business investment decisions. By understanding how this form of the process works in the commercial world, you will begin to see its potential usefulness for nonprofits.

Investors are generally conservative and careful about where they commit their resources to business opportunities. Their funds and time are limited, so they want to make informed decisions in a clear and efficient way. Due diligence focuses their effort on collecting essential information prior to making a choice. It is the structured process that helps potential investors get to know a company, its market, and its management. It is also the process a company uses to get to know potential investors.

Prior to committing to a new venture, the investor assesses the feasibility of the concept or product, the potential market, the quality of company management, and the success of its current products or services. For significant new investments, this can be a detailed review that encompasses meetings with company personnel, industry research, and possible discussions with customers or potential customers. The depth of the due diligence process also varies with the size and history of the company. Reviews are more detailed for start-up companies with unknown markets, and less so for companies with experienced management and proven products in established markets. If an investor has worked with a company for an extended period and is making an additional investment, the process can be quite simple.

Although investors understand there is no guarantee of success, the first goal of the process is to minimize or reduce the level of risk and thereby avoid failures. Among the basic questions they ask during the due diligence processes are the following:

- Does the company have an adequate business plan?

- Does the company have the infrastructure and processes it needs to operate efficiently and effectively?

- Is there a need in the market for the service or product being offered or developed?

- Does management have the ability to implement their plan, and does the plan have a reasonable chance of succeeding?

- Does management have the ability to manage the invested funds to optimize their intended use?

- Does the company maintain an adequately trained workforce? If not, are the necessary skills available in the local labor market?

- What specialized capital equipment or facilities are required for the operation?

- What is the relationship between management and the company's board of directors? Does the board truly perform an oversight function?

Simultaneously, management explores the objectives and motivations of the investor group. It reviews the investors' philosophy, approach, and history of successes and failures with other companies. It also assesses the constraints the investor will place on the company. For example, some investors require a seat on the board of directors, and others release funds only when the business meets certain performance milestones. At the conclusion of the process, which can extend from several days to several weeks of work, both the investor and the company have sufficient information to make an informed decision about proceeding.

Due Diligence in Nonprofit Decision Making

The due diligence process can provide nonprofits with a systematic way to assess key components of critical decisions. By assuming the role of an external investor, the nonprofit's leadership can address new problems or opportunities in a predictable and ordered way.

Due diligence in nonprofits becomes the process by which the decision makers carry out a self-study of their organization: its constituencies, infrastructure, and resource base. If an external party is driving the decision, as in the case of funder initiatives, it is also the method for assessing the organization's fit with the plans of the outside group.

As with commercial investments, nonprofit due diligence should address the factors necessary for success, including the feasibility of the proposed choices (minimize risk), the potential impact on various constituencies (maximize leverage), and the capacity of the organization's management and infrastructure (ensure sustainability). For major strategic decisions that potentially affect the organization's mission, such as merger with another organization, the process might be highly detailed. There might be meetings with the organization's staff and board members, sector research, detailed financial analysis and projections, and possible discussions with constituent groups. If the decision is about a limited program or administrative area and the decision makers have been with the organization for an extended period and have reliable information, the review process might be quite simple. Modifying or expanding existing programming to serve new communities or clients can fall into this category.

Parallel to the due diligence questions asked of commercial companies, the following questions would be asked of nonprofits:

- Does the organization have an adequate planning process and documentation? Strategic plans? Operational plans? Program and project plans? Assessment and evaluation processes and reports?

- Does the organization have adequate management and program capacity?

- Is there a need for the change being proposed?

- Does management have the ability to implement the decision, and does it have a reasonable chance of succeeding?

- Does management have the adequate financial resources required to implement the decision and sustain the change over time?

- Does the organization have an adequately trained workforce of staff and volunteers? If not, are the skills available in the local community?

- What specialized capital equipment or facilities are required for the new operation, project, or program?

- How does the change fit with the board's oversight function? What specific structures, processes, and policies exist that would support the decision?

If the decision is the result of an idea initiated or supported by an external party, such as a foundation and government initiative, or joint programming proposed by another nonprofit, due diligence becomes the process by which the decision makers get to know that other party. The motives, assumptions, expectations, and objectives behind the proposed change should be explored. Agendas can vary greatly among individuals, other nonprofits, private foundations, corporations, and government agencies. In addition, the decision makers should review the constraints that the external party will place on the organization. For example, a proposed program might be limited to certain communities, funders might not cover overhead associated with a proposed project, or government might require certain credentialing for program staff.

At the end of the process—which might be complex or relatively simple, depending on the scope of the decision and information available—the decision makers will be in a position to make an informed choice. The organization at this point knows the likely risks and probable outcome and can therefore proceed. If it chooses to forgo a certain course of action, the reasons will be clear. The decision makers will understand the potential long-term impact of the decision on the organization's capacity, staff, and financial resource base.

Staging Implementation to Reduce Risk

Take calculated risks. That is quite different from being rash.
—*George S. Patton*

Once the decision to proceed is made, commercial investors usually commit to resources to a business venture in phases relative to its implementation. Each phase represents a series of related decisions, moving from initial assessment to full implementation. As we previously discussed, often in reactive decision making there is a sense of urgency accompanied by a rush to put ideas into action. By intentionally slowing the implementation process and breaking a critical decision into stages, the organization is able to test the impact of the decision and the resources required. Based on the results at each stage, the decision makers can continue to proceed, learn from the results, and make needed modifications, or in some cases cut their losses and abandon the decision altogether. Staging helps to minimize risk while maximizing leverage and ensuring sustainability.

Four types of decisions correspond to the successive phases in making and implementing a critical decision in nonprofit organizations:

- Feasibility

- Pilot

- Implementation

- Cutback

Each represents a successive stage with a different level of risk and organizational commitment. Phasing critical choices mitigates the sense of urgency with the security of a structured due diligence process. Instead of being rash, you take calculated risks and know what to expect from each stage.

THE FOUR STAGES OF DECISION MAKING

Feasibility

Feasibility is the first phase in considering any critical decision. In assessing the feasibility of an idea, you ask this central question: "Can this be done?"

Nonprofits are familiar with feasibility studies associated with capital campaigns and building projects. They determine the availability of funding required for the proposed project to proceed. If sufficient funds are unavailable, a program or project is determined not to be feasible.

Applying the feasibility concept to the broad range of critical decisions facing an organization provides a way to explore the viability of a new concept, project, program, or process. This means learning what it will take to implement the project successfully before taking action.

Once an organization has carried out a thoughtful and complete feasibility assessment as the first stage in making a critical decision, it can proceed toward implementation with an understanding of the potential risks. If a choice is judged feasible, the organization is prepared to move forward to the next phase and put the decision into action through a limited test or pilot.

Pilot

Unanticipated problems can and often do emerge when decisions that can be feasible are put into action. This risk is greatly reduced by testing the decision in a pilot stage before fully implementing it. Piloting a novel decision in a nonprofit context is similar to a commercial company using a seed investment to build a product prototype or, in some cases, several prototypes. With nonprofit decisions, the pilot includes limited implementation of program or operational innovation.

At the conclusion of the pilot stage, the results should be measurable and documented and compared with the results anticipated in the feasibility stage. If the pilot is completed successfully, the organization is ready to fully implement the decision. If the pilot is not successful, the decision makers understand why, they are able to limit the negative impact of the pilot, and they are then in a position to investigate and pursue other options.

Implementation

Once the organization has demonstrated that the decision is viable by trying it out or testing it in a limited way, the decision can be implemented fully. In the commercial sector, this is analogous to rolling out a new product or service that has undergone full market testing. In nonprofits, this might include expanding a program from one site to several, taking a new administrative process from one department to the entire organization, or making a temporary activity permanent.

The implementation stage incorporates continuous monitoring of the decision in terms of its ability to enhance the organization's performance over time, so it never really ends. If any of the indicators show that the choice no longer has its intended impact or the resources required to sustain it are not available, its implementation may pose a risk to the organization. If this is the case, it might be time to enter the cutback stage.

Cutback

When established projects, processes, or infrastructure no longer adequately meet community needs or support the organization's goals, the fourth stage in the critical decision process emerges: the cutback decision, when decision makers seek to reduce or eliminate parts of the organization that are no longer working well. These can include activities, programs, administrative structures, and processes. In addition, they can include changing relationships with other organizations, divesting property and equipment, and reducing staff.

In many ways cutback decisions are similar to feasibility decisions and use a similar series of questions to demonstrate that an established activity is no longer viable. If cutbacks are carried out in a measured and strategic manner, they can position the organization to move forward. In this stage, decision makers not only assess the cuts in terms of current performance, but also look ahead to determine what their future impact might be.

A Consistent Approach to Critical Decisions

Success is more a function of consistent common sense than it is of genius.

—An Wang

Developing a consistent approach to making critical decisions requires defining the key elements in the due diligence process in more detail, reflecting the range of information to gather and review. This creates a common language to communicate clearly about the decision within the organization as well as to external stakeholders. As you will see in later chapters, these elements hold across and link together the four stages of feasibility, pilot, implementation, and cutback. Finally, a list of the key elements also acts as a checklist to ensure that information gathered to review the decision is complete.

Sixteen key elements form the building blocks of our approach. The decision matrix tool we present in Chapter Four provides a way of working with all of them in a clear and organized way.

THE SIXTEEN ELEMENTS OF THE DUE DILIGENCE PROCESS

1. Strategic Alignment

An effective decision sharpens an organization's ability to meet its specific goals and make progress toward its mission. Any proposed choice should be reviewed in terms of the organization's strategy and plans. It should advance the organization's core values, vision, mission, goals, objectives, and policies. A critical decision that is not aligned with the organization's strategy can lead to mission creep.

2. Feasibility

A feasible decision is one that can be implemented. Given the appropriate resources—human, financial, and material—is what is being proposed possible? In order to assess feasibility, the ultimate goal in making the decision should be clearly defined along with the distinct benefits. Perhaps other organizations have made similar choices successfully. If this is the case, management must review similarities and differences in order to determine if it is also possible in their organization and community.

3. Expertise

Specialized knowledge is often required in making and implementing critical decisions. The expertise must be identified and enlisted. Sometimes expertise can come from within the organization: staff and volunteers might already have the right combination of skills and experience. Sometimes the board can provide it, through the skills of individual members or the organizations they represent. And in some cases, the expertise must be secured from external sources, including borrowing it from other organizations through information- or staff-sharing arrangements or by purchasing it from outside providers. If expertise must be obtained externally, decision makers must determine if there will be sufficient transfer of knowledge for the organization to implement the decision and sustain the change without going outside again.

4. Reasonable Cost

In implementing a new idea, decision makers usually account for the direct costs, specifically those outside the normal budget required by a new activity. But they sometimes overlook the full range of indirect costs—those related to maintaining the organizational infrastructure needed to support the decision over time. They also sometimes neglect to address the potential increases or reductions. Fixed costs, such as leasing program space, do not change, but variable costs, such as staffing and supplies, can vary greatly depending on the level of activity. And finally, budgets are often based on past sunk costs that might be irrelevant going forward. In making critical decisions, decision makers should study their assumptions about the associated costs, both short and long term.

5. Fit

Any choice should be consistent with the capabilities of the organization and the needs of the community the organization serves, including clients, funders, oversight groups, and other nonprofits. Some critical decisions challenge the mission of the organization or require a significant change in programming or operations. If and how a major change will be managed within the context of community expectations and organizational operations is the key to successful and sustained implementation.

6. Measurable Impact

The expected results of the decision should be stated in a precise way that can be measured. Measurement provides an objective way of assessing the impact of the decision, both positive and negative. It provides a standard to determine anticipated and actual leverage resulting from a choice. Clear definition and measurement also provide a precise means of communicating the organization's intentions and results to its stakeholders and simplify reporting and accountability.

7. Appropriate Scope

A decision can be overly ambitious. The size and scope of the action and the resources needed to support it in some cases have the potential to overwhelm the organization. The budget for implementing the decision relative to the organization's operating budget should be carefully examined as a way of determining how much of the organization will be involved.

8. Personnel

Not only does the organization require the appropriate expertise to develop and implement a critical decision, but it also requires the appropriate human resources to sustain it over time. The organization should investigate and understand the personnel requirements, including the impact on current work if staff members or volunteers are assigned to new activities.

9. Practicality

Once decision makers consider a new idea feasible, they must think about the practicality of its implementation. Feasible decisions *can* be implemented: they are possible courses of action. Practical decisions, in contrast, *should* be implemented: they are appropriate for the organization, its community, and its resource base at the current time. This is perhaps the most difficult step in the process: moving from making the decision in principle to putting it into action. The difficult questions about the organization's capacity must be asked and answered. This task requires an assessment of the skills and expertise of staff and volunteers as well as available financial resources. If a similar decision has been implemented successfully by another nonprofit, the differences in organizations might render it impractical for the one now considering the choice.

10. Measurable Productivity

In addition to contributing to a measurable impact aligned with the organization's mission, the choice might make a contribution to the organization's productivity. The decision might result in the organization's becoming more effective or efficient, making a greater impact or better use of its resources. In some cases, initial implementation will result in an increase in productivity over time rather than immediately. Sometimes there are start-up costs and a learning curve as the organization incorporates a new program or process. Therefore, it is important to take into account both the long- and short-term effects on productivity.

11. Risk Factors

It is important at various stages in the decision and implementation process to understand what might go wrong. Management should examine factors that might prevent successful implementation of the new idea—for example, the risk of inadequate funding, inadequate staff expertise or inappropriate skills, or inadequate technology. They must also address the nonprofit version of market risk by assessing conditions external to the organization that might prevent constituents from benefiting from the decision.

12. Collaboration

Some decisions can be implemented more efficiently and effectively if other organizations are involved. Sometimes multiple organizations can work together and combine resources without compromising individual organizational goals. The nonprofit should determine if there are benefits to pursuing the decision with other organizations.

13. Broader Benefit

If the decision is implemented, there might be broader benefits that go beyond the individual organization to other stakeholder groups. In some cases, an organization might learn through its due diligence process that an idea is not feasible for it or other organizations. The nonprofit should have a way of disseminating the potential significance of the decision to benefit the wider community.

14. Financial Health

Critical decisions can affect the balance of resources within an organization. These can be represented in changes to the budget and financial health of the nonprofit in both the long and short terms. It is important that the organization understand the scope of the initial investment needed to implement a given choice and the long-term financial consequences of sustaining it.

15. Organization Development

Successful decisions contribute to the organization's growth and development. They can expand and enhance the array and quality of services and programming provided to the community. Internally, some choices can build management capacity and infrastructure, including the professional development of the staff and volunteers. The nonprofit should also address how a new idea might enhance an organization's future potential.

16. Board Oversight

The board of directors is ultimately responsible for the outcome of any organizational decision. Structures and processes at the board level should reflect clear lines of accountability. The critical choice should fit within the board's oversight and policy structure. If it is a major decision with strategic significance, the board should play an active advisory role. Finally, in some cases, board skills and connections in the community might be used to support the decision and its implementation.

Borrowing from business provides nonprofits with a due diligence process that supports making critical decisions. The guiding principles of minimizing risk, maximizing leverage, and ensuring sustainability provide guidelines for responding to challenges and opportunities. Staging implementation offers a way of slowing the process so that the organization can proceed with certainty and confidence. The sixteen key elements of critical decision making establish a framework for supporting a thorough and consistent review of the issues.

Our next step is to show you how to make the due diligence process as routine and comfortable as are habitual, recipe, and planning decisions.

3

Managing Critical Decisions

THE WHO, WHAT, AND HOW

It is best to do things systematically, since we are only human, and disorder is our worst enemy.

—Hesiod (fl. 800 B.C.)

CHAPTERS ONE AND TWO have laid the groundwork for our approach to making critical decisions. Our goal was to build a foundation based on the good decision-making practices that nonprofits and commercial organizations already use. In Chapter One, we outlined the ways nonprofits successfully address three categories of decisions: habitual, recipe, and planning. We also identified another important category that can benefit from a similar systematic approach: critical decisions, which address new, important, and risky choices. In Chapter Two, we described the due diligence process carried out by commercial investors that can help nonprofits fill this gap in their decision-making repertoire. Together the introductory chapters provide a common understanding of critical decisions and general guidelines for making them.

In this chapter, we finish building the framework by adding three other pieces that make the approach practical. First, we discuss the decision makers—the people who have the job of making the critical decisions and the roles they play. Second, we take a look inside each decision and break down the process of choice that decision makers use. Finally, we introduce the decision matrix as a way of organizing all components in a clear and consistent manner. Chapter Four follows with a detailed discussion of the matrix tool and how nonprofits can use it.

Who Decides?

Mine is the final decision. I am the decider, and I decide what is best.

—George W. Bush

We have a method for making critical decisions. Due diligence looks suitable, and staging decisions seems reasonable. But somebody actually has to make the decisions. For a method to be practical, people have to use it. Once people enter the picture, with their variety of knowledge, experience, and opinions, what looks clear in principle can become complicated in practice. The first step in making the approach workable is to be clear about who does what in the decision process, along with the roles individuals and groups will play.

GROUPS INVOLVED IN THE DECISION-MAKING PROCESS

In a critical decision, we can identify three central roles:

- Those who make the choice
- Those who inform the choice
- Those who must be informed of the choice

People Who Decide

First, the primary decision makers have the ultimate authority to make the choice and must assume the responsibility for the outcome. They can be characterized as the deciders. Their job is to weigh all the information and opinions and contemplate the potential impact of the decisions. If the decision is a good one and benefits the organization, the primary decision makers take the credit. And if it fails, they assume the blame. The nonprofit world is full of examples of nonprofit managers and leaders who have made good and bad choices. We offer some representative decisions that we feel will resonate with most of our readers. You can fill in the names of organizations or individuals who have made similar decisions in your own community.

Examples of Good Decisions

- Funders outsource some of their grant making to intermediary service organizations that have a better understanding of the grantee organizations.

- Opera companies assume the expense of "super titles" and translations to make performances more accessible to their audiences.

- Universities become financial investors in local community development to redefine traditional town-and-gown relationships.

Examples of Failed Decisions

- Organizations acquire real estate or undertake building projects that impose onerous cost and debt burdens.

- Boards of directors hire executives with the wrong skills.

- Staff introduce redundant programming that duplicates and undermines existing efforts in the community.

People Who Inform the Decision

Other people inform the decision. They have important and relevant information, expertise, or opinions, but they take no formal responsibility for the outcome. Because critical decisions represent areas where the organization has little or no previous experience, a key part of the decision-making process is to bring other knowledgeable parties into the process in an advisory role. Before making the decision, the primary decision makers use these contributions to more fully understand the situation, the range of options available to the organization, and the potential outcomes. Once again, consulting with others prior to making a decision is nothing new: good managers and leaders do it all the time. Here are some examples of how outside expertise is commonly used in nonprofits in making major decisions:

- Development consultants are called in to assess the feasibility of a capital campaign and interview possible donors to find out whether there is enough support to undertake the project.

- Prior to developing retail or fee-for-service operations, organizations consult with their attorneys and accountants to understand any tax implications.

- Prior to launching a new program, organizations convene focus groups with clients or audience members to determine if what is being considered meets the needs of the community.

In these examples, the groups that provide the information do not have the authority to make the decision, and they do not bear the responsibility for it, but they are crucial to the process. If they are not included, the organization runs a significant risk of making a poor decision.

People Who Should Be Informed About the Decision

Finally, there are those who are not the primary decision makers and do not necessarily inform the process but who should be notified once a decision is made. These are the individuals and groups the organization relies on for implementing the decision, including those within the organization whose work is shaped by the decision and stakeholders in the community who are affected. They should understand the reasons for the decision and its intended impact so they can work with the organization to make it a success. Once again, there are numerous examples:

- The effective introduction of a new computer system and software package requires that staff members be informed of why the specific systems and packages were selected, what new skills they will need to develop, and how this change will affect their jobs and the overall capacity of the organization.

- The creation of new services or programming requires informing and educating the target clients or audience about what the new offerings include, how they will be made available, and who is eligible to participate.

- When two nonprofits decide to merge, extensive internal and external communication becomes necessary. Employees and volunteers should understand the planned structure, operations, and programming of the new organization and any changes to their own jobs and reporting relationships. The expectations of the broader community—funders, groups served by the organization, related nonprofits—should be informed and managed also.

In any critical decision, identifying who exactly has each role will get the complex process off to a clear and well-organized start.

The first step is to identify the primary decision maker. Three simple questions help clarify who should assume this role:

- Who in the organization has the formal authority to make the decision and commit resources for its implementation? For example, hiring a new executive director and setting the salary and compensation is a board decision.

- Who is ultimately responsible for the decision's success or failure? How are they held accountable? In the case of major capital projects, the executive directors are usually responsible, and a number of measures are used to assess their performance and hold them accountable. These include keeping to budget, growth in programming and organizational capacity, and expanded service to the community.

- Who has the experience and expertise to make the best choice in this situation? In areas where good decision making requires highly developed technical and professional skills, individuals with those capabilities should be the key decision makers. For example, if new programming is proposed, a senior staff member with in-depth working knowledge of the field would be in the best position to decide.

With some critical decisions, a single person can be the primary decision maker, but there are often situations where a group assumes that role. In these cases, no individual has all the information or skills necessary to make and carry out the decision. For example, an executive director might have the authority to make a decision and control the appropriate resources to support its implementation, but this person might also lack the specialized programmatic or technical knowledge to make an informed choice. In these circumstances, someone with the appropriate expertise should become part of the decision-making team.

To sum up, the best primary decision makers, whether individuals or groups, have the authority to make the choice, control the resources necessary for its implementation, are held responsible with clear means of accountability, and possess the appropriate experience and expertise. Deficits in any one of these areas can lead to significant problems.

Once the primary decision maker is identified, the next step is to put together the right people to inform the process and support implementation. Keep in mind that critical decisions are complex and require new information. Stakeholder buy-in usually requires a collective effort, even when a single individual is the primary decision maker. So putting together the right team to inform the decision is important for a successful outcome.

We know a lot about what makes a group effective, as well as what might get in its way. It is widely acknowledged that participation by multiple parties can lead to better choices. But there are also potential drawbacks if the group is not managed properly. The social and political dynamics of the group can lead to dysfunctional behavior such as groupthink, and decisions may be made without needed discussion or debate.[1]

When a group approaches a critical decision, therefore, we should first clarify who will participate and in what role. The next step is to develop a shared understanding among group members of what is expected of each one and what their anticipated contribution to the process will be. In other words, everyone participating in the decision should know who is bringing what to the party.

Once we know who is responsible for what facets of the issue, the process should be structured in such a way as to allow multiple individuals to review information in a clear and consistent way. This includes capturing and comparing individual opinions and assumptions about key issues such as risk and impact. Maintaining communication and coordination throughout is a major part of managing the decision-making effort. At the end of the process, everyone involved should understand the how and why of the final decision.

What Choices?

The more alternatives, the more difficult the choice.
—Abbé D'Allanival

We have organized the people in the decision-making process in a set of coordinated roles. Now we can move on to organizing the choice itself. Once we explain the mechanics of how to make a decision, we can add another layer of organization to the process, and the decision will become more manageable.

Anyone making a choice usually has a number of options. In decision-making jargon, we call these alternative courses of action. So in principle, if you are facing a choice, you can elect to do this or you can do that or perhaps you can do the other thing. A thorough understanding of the options can go a long way in making good critical decisions.[2]

Fortunately, with critical decisions, the kinds of choices we face are quite limited. In fact, the decision maker confronts only one of three basic types:

- Binary choices
- Choices among similar options
- Choices among dissimilar options

Each category reflects the scope or complexity of the possible courses of action. A comprehensive approach to making critical decisions should address these three categories of choice, from the simplest binary decision to the most complex set of diverse trade-offs. And the method should capture the full range of options in a consistent and clear way so it will be useful for both individual and group decision making.

Binary Choices

The most limited among the three choices in scope, a binary choice means doing something or doing nothing. After reviewing the situation, the decision maker determines whether a specific course of action is to be taken: do it or don't do it. For example, a nonprofit receives a request for proposal from a funder. The activities eligible for support do not fall within the organization's current mission and do not complement future program plans. Therefore, management will most likely choose not to apply for the funding. In this case, not taking action on the request for proposal is an informed and appropriate decision. The course of action is to take no action.

Choosing Among Similar Options

Decision makers often face choosing when there are two or more similar alternatives. For example, in recruiting for an important vacant position, a manager may have an array of candidates with similar credentials and experience. Any of them would probably be a good addition to the staff. The choice would then be based on who was judged the best match for the organization. Understanding differences among options, no matter how slight, is critical in making this type of decision. Although every option might be appropriate to some extent, the best or optimal choice is the one that best fits the needs of the organization.

Choosing Among Dissimilar Options

The most complex decision situation arises when decision makers must compare and choose from two or more dissimilar options. Imagine, for example, that a nonprofit receives an unanticipated bequest of $500,000. There are several potential uses for the gift. It could be used to expand an existing successful program, or support a feasibility study for a new building, or upgrade an outdated computer system, or be set aside as a reserve fund. Unlike a situation where options are similar, here the decision maker is comparing apples with oranges. In this example, good decision making requires a consistent way to compare and assess programs, capital projects, computer systems, and reserve funds. The decision maker must go beyond the immediate impact of the options and determine which has the greatest strategic potential for supporting the organization's mission and making a significant positive impact in the community.

How Do You Put It All Together?

Everything should be made as simple as possible, but not one bit simpler.

—Albert Einstein

We now have all the pieces for a practical approach to critical decisions:

- Sixteen elements of the due diligence process

- Four stages of implementation

- Three individual or group roles

- Three types of decisions

How do we put these together to make a comprehensive model? If we take an elementary approach and add up pieces, we have 26 building blocks to consider. If we are slightly more sophisticated and look at possible combinations by multiplying them, we have 576. And once we factor in the number of people in the process, either approach can become truly onerous. But let's stop for a moment. We do have to capture the decision-making process in all its richness and complexity, but we should do so in a way that is efficient and clear to everyone. In other words, we have to make this as simple as possible but not too simple—that is, simple enough that people will actually use it.

Let's see exactly what our approach has to capture to be both complete and practical:

- It should be efficient, allowing the decision maker to respond to novel situations in a timely manner.

- It should be a routine and consistent approach across all decisions.

- It should incorporate the sixteen due diligence criteria.

- It should minimize risk through a phased approach including feasibility, pilot, implementation, and cutback.

- It should apply to both individual and group decisions.

- It should capture both subjective and objective information, facts as well as opinions.

- It should apply to all three decision types: binary, choices among similar options, and choices among dissimilar options.

- It should provide clear recording and communication of the process and the resulting decision, supporting the three decision-making roles.

There are two ways to approach the decision process using these criteria. The first is through a series of guiding questions and checklists. This approach is thorough, but it will soon become overwhelming and confusing because of the sheer amount of information and the multiple points of comparison.

It is easier to take a second approach and capture the information and process through a set of graphic tools. Using a matrix simplifies and streamlines the process. This approach relies on easy-to-interpret charts for presenting and comparing data.

The next chapter contains an overview of the matrix approach, and the rest of the book goes on to provide a step-by-step overview of how the matrix is used in a staged due diligence process for making critical decisions in nonprofits.

4

Enter the Matrix

INTRODUCING AN EFFECTIVE TOOL

Unfortunately, no one can be told what the Matrix is. You have to see it for yourself.

—Morpheus (Lawrence Fishburne), in the film The Matrix

NOW THAT WE HAVE EXPLORED what is involved in making a critical decision, the next step is to bring together and manage all the pieces of the process. Just as we've done in previous chapters, we adopt an approach that is already widely and successfully used: the decision matrix.

Matrix tools routinely support a number of different types of decisions in the commercial sector.[1] Engineers use them to evaluate design options.[2] Purchasing agents rely on them to help select vendors.[3] They are a key part of the Six Sigma method for quality assurance.[4] And as we have seen, investors often use them for evaluating possible transactions. A matrix is a graphic means of presenting and comparing multiple sets of information simultaneously and consistently, structuring the decision process and making it transparent and efficient.

This chapter is devoted to constructing an easy-to-use decision matrix for critical decisions. First, we lay out a basic framework to organize the due diligence criteria as well as the opinions of the decision makers. Then we incorporate a system for recording the importance of each of the due diligence criteria by assigning weights and scoring opinions. This provides a simple way to measure the potential impact of each decision. Finally, we demonstrate how to use the matrix in the three types of choices: binary, choices among similar options, and choices among dissimilar options. Chapters Five through Eight then provide matrices and illustrative mini-cases for each of the stages of the critical decision process: feasibility, pilot, implementation, cutback, and staff development.

The Matrix: Framing the Decision

Art consists of limitation. The most beautiful part of every picture is the frame.

—Gilbert Keith Chesterton

A matrix is a visually elegant yet simple grid: a rectangular arrangement of rows and columns. The rows represent one set of factors, the columns another. The number of rows and columns depends on the number of factors. We will use the basic matrix template presented in Exhibit 4.1 as the foundation for our decision matrix.

The two sets of factors in any critical decision are the due diligence criteria and the opinions of the decision makers. In our decision matrix, these are presented in the rows and columns. Each row contains one of the sixteen due diligence criteria. Each column in the matrix represents an individual decision maker, with the number of columns representing the number of

Exhibit 4.1. The Matrix Template.			
	Column 1	*Column 2*	*Column 3*
Row 1			
Row 2			
Row 3			

decision makers participating in the process. Each cell within the matrix—where a column and row intersect—contains the individual decision maker's opinion about that one criterion. This basic decision matrix is presented in Exhibit 4.2.

Exhibit 4.2. The Basic Decision Matrix.		
	Decision Maker 1	*Decision Maker 2*
Strategic alignment		
Feasibility		
Expertise		
Reasonable cost		
Fit		
Measurable impact		
Appropriate scope		
Personnel		
Practicality		
Measurable productivity		
Risk factors		
Collaboration		
Broader benefit		
Financial health		
Organization development		
Board oversight		

The Rows: Weighting the Due Diligence Criteria

First weigh the considerations, then take the risks.

—*Helmuth von Moltke*

Depending on the decision, the due diligence criteria can vary in importance. For example, in some cases, close board oversight and direct involvement may be necessary, whereas in others this may not be the case. If a choice is closely aligned with the strategic plan that the board developed, the board's additional oversight may be unnecessary. A simple weighting system can be used to show how important each factor is. A *weight* is the number of points assigned to each criterion. The higher the number, the heavier the weight is, and therefore the more important the factor becomes.

In our experience, certain criteria are usually given the heaviest weightings: strategic alignment, feasibility, expertise, and reasonable cost. That is because these are essential to the decision's success in the short and long terms. Others, such as collaboration and broader benefit, might enhance the outcome of the decision but are usually not critical to its success or failure; therefore, they usually receive lower weightings.

For simplicity, our critical decision matrix uses a system that divides 100 points among the criteria: more points are assigned to the most important factors and fewer points to the least important, in such a way that the total of all the points is 100. Assigning weights to the various due diligence criteria is often done best in consultation with others who understand the nature of the decision, the workings of the nonprofit organization making the decision, and the potential impact on the broader community. Exhibit 4.3 provides an example of a critical decision matrix with the due diligence weights written in. In the example, we have imagined a case where the organization has a well-developed strategic plan and the policies to support it, so direct board involvement is not very important. Therefore, we assign strategic alignment the highest number of points (18) and board oversight the lowest (1). We use these same weights throughout the chapter to make some of the comparisons clearer. In later chapters, we vary the weighting in our examples to illustrate how it can reflect the different conditions facing different organizations.

Exhibit 4.3. Sample Weighting.	
Criteria	Weight
Strategic alignment	18
Feasibility	14
Expertise	10
Reasonable cost	10
Fit	10
Measurable impact	8
Appropriate scope	5
Personnel	4
Practicality	4
Measurable productivity	4
Risk factors	4
Collaboration	2
Broader benefit	2
Financial health	2
Organization development	2
Board oversight	1
Total	**100**

The Columns: Scoring the Due Diligence Criteria

If winning isn't everything, why do they keep score?

—*Vince Lombardi*

Each row in the decision matrix represents one of the weighted due diligence criteria, and each column represents one decision maker. The rows and columns intersect to form a grid. Each box, or cell, in the grid is used to record how a specific decision maker assesses or scores each of the criteria. In this way, the matrix provides a way of collecting and presenting individual opinions about all the elements of a critical choice in a format where they can be compared easily.

The scoring system is set up as simply as possible: people record their preferences on a straightforward 0-to-10-point scale. The lowest score, 0, is assigned if a criterion is not met at all. The highest score, 10, indicates that the criterion is met fully. Scores in between, from 1 to 9, indicate that the criteria are met to a lesser or greater degree.

Let's take an elementary example and assume that the successful implementation of a mentoring program for teenaged boys requires significant expertise in youth development. "Expertise" will therefore be a heavily weighted criterion in deciding whether to implement the program. The decision maker will evaluate the expertise available to the nonprofit on a scale of 1 to 10. If there is no youth development expertise in the organization or readily available in the community, the score might be 0. But if the organization has a youth development specialist on staff who has worked in highly successful mentoring programs, the score might be 10. Scores in between indicate reservations or questions. For instance, if there is concern whether existing staff can take on new commitments, the scoring for expertise might be reduced to 8. Each of these numbers—0, 10, and 8—reflects how well a decision maker thinks the choice to implement meets the due diligence criteria.

Each decision maker uses an individual scoring grid with spaces for comments next to the criteria to record the reasons for their scores. Recording the commentary is especially important because it captures the information and opinions of the decision makers. At later points in the process, these can be compared and discussed to build a shared understanding of the issues and create consensus. Exhibit 4.4 provides a sample individual scoring sheet. In

Exhibit 4.4. Sample Individual Scoring Sheet.		
Criteria	*Individual Scores*	*Comments*
Strategic alignment	10	Meets major goal in current strategic plan
Feasibility	3	Was tried in another city but no evaluation
Expertise	6	Some staff expertise— but we'd have to hire a consultant too
Reasonable cost	0	The project budget is 50% of our annual budget—no way!
Fit	5	Fits our organizational goals—but we would need more space/staff
Measurable impact	7	Clear measures—but no processes proposed
Appropriate scope	2	Way too ambitious—could overwhelm the organization
Personnel	5	Staff have knowledge, but we would need considerable outside help
Practicality	0	This is too ambitious for us at the present time
Measurable productivity	8	Measures are clear—but we wouldn't see increase for 3 to 5 years
Risk factors	0	Too risky in terms of dollars and staff time
Collaboration	8	Opportunity to collaborate with another good organization
Broader benefit	8	If successful results could be measured and disseminated
Financial health	1	Without significant new funding, financial health is seriously jeopardized
Organization development	3	Would develop the organization in only one program area
Board oversight	2	Not enough board oversight given the level of financial risk

the example, the decision maker feels strongly that the decision is aligned with the organization's strategy and has scored that criterion a 10, but the program is cost prohibitive, so he has given that criterion a 0. He also has questions about the other criteria, and this is reflected in the different scores and the reasoning behind them in the Comments column.

In situations with multiple decision makers, each can individually evaluate the decision first using the scoring grids; then the results can be consolidated onto one grid and the individual scores for the criteria compared, reviewed, and discussed systematically. Exhibit 4.5 provides an example of how three decision makers might individually score the same decision.

The example in Exhibit 4.5 illustrates the differences in how individuals can evaluate and score the same decision situation. Some individuals can be critical in their assessment and systematically assign low scores when grading. Others can be very optimistic and be consistently high scorers. Still others assign a wide range of scores because they tend to see clear distinctions. In this example, decision maker 1 gives mostly high scores, while decision maker 2 assigns mostly low ones. Decision maker 3 uses the broadest range of scores, with some very low and others extremely high. The matrix accommodates the style of each decision maker and before the scores are weighted allows true agreement and disagreement to surface. For example, decision maker 3 rated reasonable cost a 0, while decision makers 1 and 2 gave it high scores. They are in general agreement about all other criteria. Perhaps decision maker 3 knows more about the costs associated with the project than decision makers 1 and 2, or vice versa. Whatever is driving the difference, the matrix indicates that the decision makers should discuss cost at greater length so they can reach a better understanding of the information. We should note that there are situations where decision makers can disagree with each other profoundly. These situations can become uncomfortable and politically charged. In cases like these, the matrix will get them only so far: it will help record and clarify the various points of view, but reaching a consensus is dependent on the group members' willingness and ability to negotiate.

The total score for each criterion is calculated by adding the individual scores. This sum is recorded in a box to the right of the grid. The total weighted score for each factor is then calculated by multiplying the total score by the

Exhibit 4.5. Sample Consolidated Scoring Sheet.			
Criteria	Decision Maker 1	Decision Maker 2	Decision Maker 3
Strategic alignment	9	6	8
Feasibility	5	2	3
Expertise	7	4	6
Reasonable cost	10	7	0
Fit	7	3	5
Measurable impact	8	5	7
Appropriate scope	4	1	2
Personnel	6	4	5
Practicality	2	0	0
Measurable productivity	10	7	8
Risk factors	3	1	0
Collaboration	9	7	10
Broader benefit	8	5	8
Financial health	2	0	1
Organization development	6	2	3
Board oversight	9	7	10
Totals	**105**	**61**	**76**

weight given to the specific criterion. The total weighted score is recorded in a box to the right of the total score. Exhibit 4.6 provides an illustration using the same decision presented in Exhibit 4.5.

The total score provides a measure of the decision makers' collective judgment that the choice meets specific criteria. The higher the score, the better the match. In Exhibit 4.6, with three decision makers, a perfect total score for any one of the criteria would be 30. That is, each of the three would rate that factor with the highest possible score, 10. In the example, none of the criteria receive a perfect total score. Two criteria receive a highest total score of 26: collaboration and board oversight. None of the criteria were considered completely unmet, and so none receive a score of 0. But practicality is close, with a total score of only 2.

Not all criteria are equally important to the decision process. Some carry more weight than others. In the example, strategic alignment has the highest weight of 18, and board oversight has the lowest, 1. The weighted total score indicates how closely the decision matches what is important for the organization: board oversight has a higher total score with 26 than strategic alignment with 23. However, once weighting has been factored in, strategic alignment outweighs board oversight with a total weighted score of 414 compared to 26.

Weighted scores also provide a way to capture the overall risk associated with a choice. This is done by first taking the sum of the total weighted scores (the score resulting from adding up the total weighted scores for all the criteria). The total possible weighted score—the score if all the decision makers gave each criterion a perfect score of 10—acts as a comparison point. In the example, the total possible weighted score is 3,000. Dividing the sum of the total weighted scores by the total possible weighted score provides a percentage of agreement. Exhibit 4.7 shows a complete matrix for the decision. The total possible weighted score is 3,000, the sum of the total weighted scores is 1,571, and agreement with the decision criteria is 52 percent. The higher the percentage, the more closely the decision meets the due diligence criteria and the lower the risk. The decision makers view this choice as having a slightly better than even chance of success or failure. If this course of action is pursued, it poses considerable risk to the organization. The lowest total scores for specific due diligence criteria indicate the areas where the risk will most likely occur.

Exhibit 4.6. Consolidated Matrix Including Total Weighted Scores.						
Criteria	Weight	Decision Maker 1	Decision Maker 2	Decision Maker 3	Total Score	Total Weighted Score
Strategic alignment	18	9	6	8	23	414
Feasibility	14	5	2	3	10	140
Expertise	10	7	4	6	17	170
Reasonable cost	10	10	7	0	17	170
Fit	10	7	3	5	15	150
Measurable impact	8	8	5	7	20	160
Appropriate scope	5	4	1	2	7	35
Personnel	4	6	4	5	15	60
Practicality	4	2	0	0	2	8
Measurable productivity	4	10	7	8	25	100
Risk factors	4	3	1	0	4	16
Collaboration	2	9	7	10	26	52
Broader benefit	2	8	5	8	21	42
Financial health	2	2	0	1	3	6
Organization development	2	6	2	3	11	22
Board oversight	1	9	7	10	26	26

Exhibit 4.7. Matrix with Total Weighted Scores, Total Possible Weighted Scores, and Percentage Agreement.

Criteria	Weight	Decision Maker 1	Decision Maker 2	Decision Maker 3	Total Score	Total Weighted Score
Strategic alignment	18	9	6	8	23	414
Feasibility	14	5	2	3	10	140
Expertise	10	7	4	6	17	170
Reasonable cost	10	10	7	0	17	170
Fit	10	7	3	5	15	150
Measurable impact	8	8	5	7	20	160
Appropriate scope	5	4	1	2	7	35
Personnel	4	6	4	5	15	60
Practicality	4	2	0	0	2	8
Measurable productivity	4	10	7	8	25	100
Risk factors	4	3	1	0	4	16
Collaboration	2	9	7	10	26	52
Broader benefit	2	8	5	8	21	42
Financial health	2	2	0	1	3	6
Organization development	2	6	2	3	11	22
Board oversight	1	9	7	10	26	26
Totals	**100**	**105**	**61**	**76**	**242**	**1,571**
Total possible weighted score						**3,000**
Percentage agreement						**52%**

As the example shows, the matrix provides a way to present all the critical details of a decision on one page. The due diligence criteria, their relative importance, and the decision makers' opinions are explicit and easy to compare. Capturing this information makes it possible to thoroughly assess the potential benefits or risks of a proposed action. This basic tool can be configured to support the three types of decision situations described in the previous chapter: binary choices, choices among similar options, and choices among dissimilar options.

USING THE MATRIX FOR THE THREE TYPES OF DECISIONS

Using the Matrix for Binary Decisions

Deal or no deal.

—Howie Mandel, from the television show of the same name

Binary choices can be viewed as the simplest form of action. The decision maker chooses between taking a specific course of action or doing nothing. They are often characterized as go versus no-go decisions. The amount of perceived benefit versus perceived risk is the basis of the decision. In these situations, a single matrix can be used. Exhibit 4.8 illustrates two decision makers reviewing the feasibility of a potential course of action. The percentage of agreement, 83 percent, is high, so it is viewed as potentially a successful choice. In this case, the group might decide that the action is indeed feasible and the decision is to move ahead.

Exhibit 4.9 represents a potential choice with a very low percentage of agreement: 18 percent. To generate a score this low, the decision makers must give low scores to the most heavily weighted or most important decision criteria. This is clearly a risky option. In this case, unless the group just wanted to assume the risk for some special reason, they would most likely decide to take no action. It would be a no-go.

It is important to remember that the numbers do not drive the decision. The numbers merely reflect the opinions of the decision makers. There may well be reasons that, in some cases, the decision makers will elect to

Criteria	Weight	Decision Maker 1	Decision Maker 2	Total Score	Total Weighted Score
Exhibit 4.8. Binary Decision with a High Percentage of Agreement.					
Strategic alignment	18	9	8	17	306
Feasibility	14	8	8	16	224
Expertise	10	9	9	18	180
Reasonable cost	10	10	9	19	190
Fit	10	8	9	17	170
Measurable impact	8	8	8	16	128
Appropriate scope	5	7	8	15	75
Personnel	4	9	8	17	68
Practicality	4	9	7	16	64
Measurable productivity	4	10	7	17	68
Risk factors	4	7	7	14	56
Collaboration	2	7	6	13	26
Broader benefit	2	6	6	12	24
Financial health	2	8	9	17	34
Organization development	2	7	5	12	24
Board oversight	1	9	9	18	18
Totals	**100**	**131**	**123**	**254**	**1,655**
Total possible weighted score					**2,000**
Percentage agreement					**83%**

		Decision Maker 1	Decision Maker 2	Total Score	Total Weighted Score
Exhibit 4.9. Binary Decision with a Low Percentage of Agreement.					
Criteria	Weight				
Strategic alignment	18	1	0	1	18
Feasibility	14	2	3	5	70
Expertise	10	2	2	4	40
Reasonable cost	10	0	0	0	0
Fit	10	3	2	5	50
Measurable impact	8	3	3	6	48
Appropriate scope	5	2	1	3	15
Personnel	4	4	3	7	28
Practicality	4	0	0	0	0
Measurable productivity	4	3	2	5	20
Risk factors	4	1	1	2	8
Collaboration	2	9	8	17	34
Broader benefit	2	5	4	9	18
Financial health	2	0	0	0	0
Organization development	2	4	0	4	8
Board oversight	1	2	2	4	4
Totals	**100**	**41**	**31**	**72**	**361**
Total possible weighted score					**2,000**
Percentage agreement					**18%**

pursue a risky course of action. For example, the decision in Exhibit 4.9 scores high on Collaboration. Perhaps in reviewing the scoring, the decision makers agree that the opportunity to work with another group is worth the risk and might provide benefits or options for the organization in the future. The purpose of the matrix and scoring system is to provide a clear record of the potential benefits and risks and thus to inform the decision process.

Using the Matrix for Choices Among Similar Options

> *There's no business like show business, but there are several businesses like accounting.*
>
> —*David Letterman*

The matrix can also be useful in deciding between two or more similar options. In this case, each option is given its own matrix and is evaluated separately by the decision makers. When the total weighted scores for each choice are compared, the least risky option emerges.

When we set the summary matrices for each choice side by side, we see the similarities and differences. With truly similar options, the matrices should reflect agreement on numerous criteria and disagreement on a few. In cases where all the options are strong, similar options will have similar scores on the most heavily weighted criteria; the differences will be reflected in the less important ones.

Exhibit 4.10 provides a summary matrix of how a decision maker scores two similar options. The scoring on the most heavily weighted and important criteria are almost identical for both. Option 2 scores high on the less heavily weighted criteria as well and is therefore the stronger choice.

Using the Matrix for Choices Among Dissimilar Options

> *There's a difference between a philosophy and a bumper sticker.*
>
> —*Charles M. Schulz*

The process for treating different options—comparing apples to oranges—is the same as the process used for treating similar options. When we introduced

			Option 1		Option 2
Criteria	Weight	Option 1 Score	Score Weighted	Option 2 Score	Score Weighted
Exhibit 4.10. Matrix Comparing Similar Options.					
Strategic alignment	18	9	162	9	162
Feasibility	14	10	140	10	140
Expertise	10	7	70	8	80
Reasonable cost	10	9	90	9	90
Fit	10	8	80	9	90
Measurable impact	8	10	80	10	80
Appropriate scope	5	8	40	9	45
Personnel	4	8	32	8	32
Practicality	4	9	36	8	32
Measurable productivity	4	8	32	9	36
Risk factors	4	10	40	10	40
Collaboration	2	2	4	9	18
Broader benefit	2	2	4	8	16
Financial health	2	5	10	9	18
Organization development	2	3	6	7	14
Board oversight	1	2	2	10	10
Totals	**100**	**110**	**828**	**142**	**903**
Total possible weighted score			**1,000**		**1,000**
Percentage agreement			**83%**		**90%**

this type of decision, we gave an example of an organization that received an unanticipated bequest and had a number of diverse ways this money could be put to use. In cases like this, each possible choice is given its own matrix and is ranked independently. The scores for each option can be consolidated and compared in a side-by-side format. The total weighted score is then used to determine which option most closely matches the decision criteria and is therefore the most beneficial and least risky. The option with the highest total weighted score is the most desirable choice.

Exhibit 4.11 provides a summary matrix of how a decision maker scores two different options. Unlike Exhibit 4.10 where the similarities between the options are reflected in similar scoring on most of the criteria, there is almost no similarity in scoring in Exhibit 4.11. This is what we expect when different options have different strengths and weaknesses in terms of risks and benefits. In Exhibit 4.11, the decision maker assesses that option 1 meets most of the important or heavily weighted criteria and is somewhat weaker on the less important ones. Option 2 scores well on only a few of the criteria. Option 1 is therefore the better choice, and this is reflected in the total weighted scores and percentage agreement for each option, with option 1 rating at 81 percent and option 2 at 52 percent.

———————

In making critical decisions, it is essential to capture all the relevant information and opinions in a way that is clear, consistent, and easily managed. Now that you have been introduced to the matrix you can see that a visual display can both anchor and facilitate the decision-making process. At this point, it might be helpful if you work with the matrix for a bit and use it to revisit one or two of your more or less successful decision-making experiences. Or you might develop a hypothetical decision situation and test it with someone. In this way, you can become more comfortable and skilled at working with this tool. Once you're comfortable with the matrix, look at how the weighting system might be different in your organization. Which due diligence criteria carry the most weight, and why? Perhaps you are facing financial challenges, so financial health might merit greater weight. Or perhaps you are in the midst of significant change, and the board is more directly

Criteria	Weight	Option 1 Score	Option 1 Score Weighted	Option 2 Score	Option 2 Score Weighted
Exhibit 4.11. Matrix Comparing Two Different Options.					
Strategic alignment	18	8	144	6	108
Feasibility	14	10	140	8	112
Expertise	10	10	100	8	80
Reasonable cost	10	5	50	2	20
Fit	10	7	70	7	70
Measurable impact	8	10	80	2	16
Appropriate scope	5	7	35	3	15
Personnel	4	10	40	9	36
Practicality	4	7	28	4	16
Measurable productivity	4	8	32	8	32
Risk factors	4	8	32	2	8
Collaboration	2	2	4	0	0
Broader benefit	2	9	18	0	0
Financial health	2	5	10	0	0
Organization development	2	8	16	2	4
Board oversight	1	6	6	3	3
Totals	**100**	**120**	**805**	**64**	**520**
Total possible weighted score			**1,000**		**1,000**
Percentage agreement			**81%**		**52%**

involved in the process. In that case, board oversight might be assigned more weight and other criteria, such as collaboration and broader benefit, less.

It has been our experience that nonprofit managers quickly become adept at using the matrix to compile information and support discussion and find it a useful record-keeping and communication tool as well. In the next four chapters, we develop matrices for the four decision types: feasibility, pilot, implementation, and cutback. We discuss the appropriate inclusion and weighting of the diligence criteria at each stage and provide brief illustrative cases based on actual decisions nonprofits have made.

PART 2

Making Critical Decisions

5

Stage One: Feasibility

*Nothing is impossible. Some things are
just less likely than others.*

—Jonathan Winters

THE FIRST STAGE of the due diligence process, feasibility, is
intended to determine before any action is taken on a new idea how
likely it is that the idea might succeed or fail. Information and opinions
about potential risks and benefits are gathered, reviewed, and evaluated.
With a structured way of assessing a proposed action before committing to
implementation, management can more fully realize the benefits of a good
decision and avoid the damage caused by a bad one.

This chapter builds on the due diligence process outlined in Chapter
Two. It begins with a reminder of how individuals and organizations can
react to new situations and ideas. With this introduction—or warning,
depending on how you look at it—we underscore the importance of determining whether a concept is feasible before rushing to implement it. Second,
this chapter outlines major feasibility decisions common to nonprofits. We
would venture to guess that most of you have had experience with similar
decisions and so can draw on actual and personal examples that can help
illustrate different points in assessing feasibility. Third, the chapter presents
the feasibility matrix based on the criteria discussed in Chapter Three, along

with detailed guidelines for scoring. The chapter concludes with two illustrative minicases.

The Seductive Nature of New Ideas

Let's have some new clichés!
—Samuel Goldwyn

New ideas are often exciting and compelling. Whether they emerge in response to external pressures or are the result of individual creativity, they can be a strong force for organizational change. Enthusiasm for a new idea creates the momentum to carry it forward to action. Reactive decision making, with all its pitfalls, results if the excitement is not tempered with objective and thoughtful evaluation.

Because new ideas represent uncharted territory for an organization, implementing them without careful review can pose significant risks. By taking the time to examine the potential benefits and possible problems, management assumes a responsive position. With a more complete understanding of what the proposal entails, negative consequences can be avoided and positive ones enhanced. Balance is the key. When you maintain the subjective emotional connection with a creative idea while tempering it with objective facts and data, you ensure that your commitment will be supported by a deeper understanding of the idea's potential. The result is a well-informed decision.

Deciding whether an idea is feasible is the first step in due diligence. For a relatively modest investment of time, organizations can reasonably assess the viability of a novel suggestion in terms of risk, leverage, and sustainability before it's put into practice. This approach goes a long way toward limiting risk. Many innovative ideas that at first appear to have great potential become questionable on closer review. For example, a new program might require more resources to implement and sustain than the organization can afford, or it might replicate established programs that already adequately meet community needs.

A thorough feasibility assessment can enhance a viable idea and increase its leverage, that is, its benefit to the organization and community for the resources invested. For example, in the course of reviewing costs and impact, management might discover that the original scope of a proposed program should be expanded because the demand is actually much greater than originally assumed.

Finally, new ideas often address immediate issues or opportunities and therefore focus on the short term. It is important to understand how an innovation will contribute to the organization over time. If an idea is truly feasible, its impact will be sustainable in the long term and contribute to organizational stability. For example, an investment in new computer technology might result in enough increased productivity to support its ongoing maintenance and improvement. In contrast, the acquisition of a new building might impose a significant debt burden on the organization and strain its financial resources for many years.

Evaluating the feasibility of an idea before committing to implementation provides a structured process to determine exactly how the innovation might lead to success or failure. The feasibility evaluation should answer two questions: first, the general question, "Can this be done?" and, second, if it can be done, "Can this organization do it?"

Common Feasibility Decisions

Friends have all things in common.

—Plato

Several common categories of ideas are frequently proposed in nonprofit organizations: building projects, new programs, new technology, and responses to funder initiatives. Most of you have had experience with at least one of these and some with several. As we go through the development of the feasibility matrix, it will be helpful if you revisit your own experience with a common feasibility decision to see how you treated the various due diligence criteria. This will give you some practice working with the tool, as well as perhaps learning a little bit more about why a past project was a success or had problems.

Building Projects

Acquiring or building new facilities represents a major undertaking for non-profits. Unless ownership is critical to the mission of the nonprofit, as in the case of shelter for the homeless, it might not be the most appropriate course of action. However, building projects generate considerable enthusiasm and emotional buy-in. Bricks and mortar are attractive to many donors because they provide a tangible result. Also, ownership of a facility is often a signal to the staff, board, and community that the nonprofit is permanent and stable.

Building projects represent some of the riskiest innovations that nonprof-its undertake. It is not unusual for a small community organization with an operating budget of $200,000 to take on a multimillion-dollar capital project with no internal expertise about building design, construction, or facilities management. The financial risk is considerable. In addition, an organization often fails to look at the precise role of the new building in supporting the nonprofit's mission and enhancing its programming. The impact of the facil-ity on the organization's ability to provide programs and services to the com-munity is rarely assessed carefully. Therefore, the leverage of many building projects—their ability to provide more benefits compared to their cost—is highly questionable.

Indeed, in the long term, the funds and expertise required to service con-struction debt or maintain the facilities over time might drain resources that could otherwise go to programming. Serious questions of sustainability arise when more funds go to overhead and less to serving the community. Because the scope and impact of building projects can be substantial, it is critical to assess their overall feasibility. This goes beyond the fundraising feasibility studies discussed earlier in Chapter Three. The projects should be reviewed in terms of their overall contribution to the nonprofit's organizational performance, including contribution to the mission and programs, as well as the long-term effects on its resource base.

New Programs

Nonprofit organizations strive to be responsive to their communities. As a result, constituents request expanded services, and staff generate proposals for new programs. Staff is often willing to take on more work to serve the community. Many times, though, the impact of expanded activity is not thoroughly assessed. The actual market for the program or service, its cost, and the strain on human resources are not fully explored.

Introducing new programming without determining its strategic impact can also lead to mission creep and internal coordination problems. For example, if an organization is focused on serving children and introduces a program that serves young adults, the organization begins to drift away from its resident skill sets, knowledge base, and overall role in the community. Also, because new activities are often undertaken without directly addressing the organization's overall program mix, the organization can be working at cross-purposes with itself. For example, a department devoted to direct service might develop a training program without realizing that the education department in the same organization is developing something similar.

No matter how modest a new activity might seem, if an organization wants to maintain its programmatic integrity and staff focus, it must have a means of assessing a proposal's internal and external impact. Moreover, understanding the feasibility of a new program before it is implemented provides a basis for allocating the nonprofit's limited human resources in a way that best serves the community.

New Technology

Electronic technology supports program and administrative activities, and it can greatly increase organizational efficiency and effectiveness by providing accurate and timely information as well as improving communication. However, this technology continues to evolve rapidly, and hardware, software, and the related training can quickly become obsolete. Dealing with technological innovation is an ongoing challenge for management.

Understanding the advantages and limits of these systems for a given organization requires specialized technical knowledge, an area where many nonprofit organizations lack the necessary expertise internally. As a result, they often overlook the costs of training and ongoing maintenance of the system. Lack of integration with existing work processes can often pose risks and undermine sustainability. In these situations, outside expertise is often critical to assessing feasibility.

Funder Initiatives

External groups sometimes propose new ideas. Some funders—institutional, government, and individual—will support only feasibility studies or the initial implementation of programs and activities. Initiative funding is intended as risk capital that allows nonprofits to experiment with new ideas and assess their viability. The grantees are usually required to seek other sources of funding to sustain the innovation.

When funder initiatives are used to support changes that have already been planned in detail, they are an extremely valuable source of funding for innovation. For example, if an organization has decided through its strategic planning process to add outreach components to programming, initiative funding targeted for new outreach activities are a good match. The organization will have already developed a solid understanding of the resources required and the anticipated impact on the community.

However, nonprofits do not always match funder initiatives with existing strategic priorities. In some cases, they will apply for funds to explore an idea without thoroughly evaluating it. As a result, they budget the resources required to initiate and sustain the activity inappropriately. And they fail to develop a comprehensive evaluation plan tied to measurable outcomes, so they cannot determine the potential leverage of the project. Although initiative funding offsets financial risk at the beginning, it can open the organization to greater risk in the long term, both financially and in terms of unintended consequences.

Initiative funding can also come with significant political considerations. Nonprofits strive to maintain good relationships with funders. If a funder initiative presents an opportunity to build a relationship, turning it down can

be difficult. The situation is especially delicate if a funder targets specific organizations and invites them to participate. A thorough and clear process for
evaluating feasibility is critical in these situations. An organization can use the
findings of a thorough feasibility assessment as the basis for a dialogue with
the funder. The assessment will enable the decision makers to discuss in detail
why a funding opportunity is appropriate or poses potential problems.

The Feasibility Matrix

*Victorious warriors win first and then go to war, while
defeated warriors go to war first and then seek to win.*
—*Sun Tzu*, **The Art of War, Strategic Assessments**

A feasibility matrix based on the model in Chapter Four provides a decision
support tool for new ideas. The feasibility matrix in Exhibit 5.1 incorporates
all the due diligence criteria from Chapter Three to provide a comprehensive
initial assessment of a proposed idea. The format allows any number of decision makers to assess a new idea and record their opinions with a weighted
ranking system. The weighting of each criterion is determined by the key
decision makers prior to the assessment. The more heavily weighted the criterion is, the more important it is in minimizing risk, maximizing leverage,
and ensuring sustainability of the outcome. Each decision maker ranks each
of the criteria on a scale of 0 to 10.

The decision makers can be guided in their rankings by the questions set
forth below. If the decision maker has all the necessary information and can
answer the questions precisely with the specific information available, the
score on that criterion will be higher. If the decision maker cannot answer
the questions or if the answers do not support the decision criterion, the
score will be lower.

Strategic Alignment

In most cases, a new idea should clearly complement an organization's current
strategy: its plans for the future reflected in its values, vision, mission, program

Exhibit 5.1. Sample Individual Feasibility Matrix.

Criteria	Weight	Decision Maker Score	Weighted Score
Strategic alignment			
Feasibility			
Expertise			
Reasonable cost			
Fit			
Measurable impact			
Appropriate scope			
Personnel			
Practicality			
Measurable productivity			
Risk factors			
Collaboration			
Broader benefit			
Financial health			
Organization development			
Board oversight			
Totals	**100**		
Total possible weighted score			**1,000**
Percentage agreement			**%**

and organizational goals, and allocation of resources. An organization's important areas of activity are outlined and prioritized in its strategic planning documents. The best innovations are those that support and advance the organization's highest-priority action items in significant ways. Problems arise when novel ideas do not clearly fit within the organization's strategy and divert resources to areas that do not support the organization's mission or goals.

If a new idea challenges the organization's strategic plan, it is not necessarily inappropriate. There are times when major changes are proposed that make leadership rethink the organization's role and general strategy. Fortunately, this does not happen very often. If a new idea falls into this category and is compelling enough to merit serious consideration, the organization should review its role and function and, if warranted, develop a comprehensive new organizational plan.

Questions to Ask to Assess Strategic Alignment

☑ How specifically does the new idea support the organization's current role in the community, reflected in its mission, goals, and values?

☑ How does the new idea fit within the organization's existing strategic and operating plans? Which specific goals and activities does it support? How specifically will it support them?

☑ What is the potential strategic impact of the new idea? That is, does it significantly contribute to the organization's ability to pursue major high-priority action items that will have a large effect on the organization overall? Or will it only marginally contribute to minor low-priority items that affect only specific programs or departments?

Once the decision makers understand in detail how a proposal will complement the organization's plans, they score its strategic alignment. The better the fit and the greater the potential positive impact on advancing the strategy, the higher the score will be.

Feasibility

Novelty depends on context. Very few ideas are truly new; most innovations are ideas that have been implemented elsewhere. There is a greater likelihood of success if an idea has already been adopted and demonstrated to be successful by other groups. And the more widespread the idea is in practice, the greater the chance that it will work in similar situations.

The decision makers should research the proposed innovation to determine if and how it has worked in other organizations.

Questions to Ask to Assess Feasibility

☑ Has anyone ever done this before? If the answer is no, here is a point where the decision maker might ask, "Why not?" An answer of yes calls for a more detailed review of the features and benefits of the idea's implementation in other organizations. In particular, the decision makers should look at how the similarities and differences in their own organization might support or undermine the new idea. For example, are there differences in human and financial resources or in the community served?

☑ Given appropriate financial and human resources, can the project be implemented? In situations where there have been no similar projects and the proposal represents a new idea, developing a detailed sense of the anticipated impact, with the features and benefits spelled out, provides a basis for understanding how feasible it might be. The decision makers might work through a series of what-if scenarios to determine if the idea makes sense or seems possible. For example, if the idea is implemented, what would its impact be on staffing, development activities, space allocation, budgets, and so on?

High scores result if the idea has been successfully implemented in similar situations and the resources to implement it in the decision makers' organization are available.

Expertise

New ideas mean introducing new knowledge and skills into an organization. Unless its people have or can get this knowledge or these skills, successful implementation will be undermined. Therefore, another important factor in determining whether an idea is feasible is to assess the needed expertise and how it will be used.

In many cases, organizations can underestimate the sophistication and specialized expertise required to manage a new idea. Current staff might be asked to master new areas for which they have neither aptitude nor interest. The result is often frustrating, inefficient, and ineffective.

Questions to Ask to Assess Expertise

☑ What kind of specialized expertise is necessary? Develop a detailed inventory of the knowledge or skills needed to implement the idea.

☑ Is the expertise already present within the organization? That is, has someone on staff demonstrated the capability at the appropriate level to support implementation of the new idea? *Demonstrated* is the key word. Often aptitude and interest are equated with ability, but they are not the same. Experience working in an area provides the practical knowledge essential to successful implementation.

☑ If the expertise must be obtained from outside the organization, where will it come from? The decision makers must determine the most appropriate source. In some cases, the board might be tapped to provide it, through either the skills of individual members or the organizations they represent. Sometimes expertise can be borrowed from other organizations, as with executive-on-loan programs. Finally, expertise can be purchased on a fee-for-service basis through temporary staffing arrangements or consulting agreements. In this case, the decision makers should determine sources for contract expertise and the associated costs.

☑ If the expertise must be obtained from outside the organization, will there be sufficient transfer of knowledge for the organization to implement the innovation without going to the outside again? The decision makers should assess what is realistically required to develop and train staff, along with the cost. In some cases, an ongoing relationship with an external provider might be necessary. They must address in detail the contracting arrangements, the costs, and how the relationship will be managed.

The more readily available the expertise and the easier it is to transfer the knowledge to the organization, the higher the decision makers' scores will be.

Reasonable Cost

Understanding how much the new idea will cost to implement and sustain is critical to assessing its feasibility. Many good ideas can be prohibitively expensive. Nonprofits often systematically under budget for new ideas. Any proposed innovation should be accompanied by a comprehensive analysis of the full range of costs and budget projections.

Questions to Ask to Assess Cost

☑ What are all the costs associated with initiating and sustaining this proposed idea? Develop a budget that includes direct and indirect costs, fixed and variable costs, and sunk versus relevant future costs. A clearly detailed narrative should accompany the budget explaining the reasons for each line.

☑ Are the budgeted amounts realistic? Review the assumptions behind the figures in each budget line. For example, if a new program requires contracting with an external consultant, how are the consultant fees calculated? If they represent a best guess based on figures from a similar project several years ago, they might be inaccurate. However, if they are based on a proposal directly from the consultant for the specified work, they will be current and realistic.

☑ Where will the resources budgeted for the innovation come from? Each line item should be tied to a reliable source of funds. If an item depends on current income streams and existing resources, will the organization's activities that are traditionally funded from these sources be affected? If the innovation is dependent on new dollars, has this money been secured? If not, what are the potential sources of funding and the time line for developing adequate support? What are the contingencies if the new sources do not materialize?

The better the decision makers know the range of costs involved and the more confidence they have in the accuracy of the budget, the higher the score will be.

Fit

The decision makers must look at the anticipated internal and external organizational impacts. This includes assessing the decision's effects, positive and negative, on existing programs and operations. In addition, the decision makers should determine whether the proposed changes are at odds with current or future trends and plans in the broader nonprofit community.

In terms of internal operations, it is critical to know how and when the innovation will be integrated. Any new activity can stress the organization. Scheduling changes, reassignment of staff, or any modifications to routine processes can degrade performance. Decision makers should plan carefully to smooth the impact of implementation.

Addressing the potential impact on the broader community is also important. Decision makers should include the relevant external stakeholder groups: clients or audience, other nonprofits, and funders; explore how to manage the change so the ultimate consumers of the organization's programming receive the maximum benefits; and think about the impact on other nonprofit providers of programming or services. New activities can be redundant or can be complementary, fostering cooperation or resulting in competition between organizations. The final issue is to address the fit between funder goals and available monies to ensure resources to support and sustain the effort.

Questions to Ask to Assess Fit

☑ How does the proposed innovation fit within the organization's annual operating plans? Besides overall strategic alignment, the innovation's fit with specific program, department, and administrative goals should be reviewed. Who will be required to implement the new idea, and how will it affect their workload? Detail any other resources that might be required, such as space and equipment, as well as the impact of allocating them for the new activity as opposed to their current use. Finally, review the proposed timing of the innovation in terms of the organization's routine activity levels.

☑ How does the new activity affect the community? Answering this question requires careful examination of the needs of the clients or audience in order to determine how and to what degree the proposed changes will serve them. Review existing and planned activity in other organizations to understand the potential for redundancy and competition, as well as for complementarity. Assess the range of funding opportunities in a similar way to increase the likelihood of sufficient support.

The better the fit is with internal operations and external stakeholders, the higher the decision makers' score will be.

Measurable Impact

Measurement is critical in assessing whether the innovation is effective and to what degree. Using quantitative and qualitative measures, the organization can determine how much bang for the buck it can reasonably expect. Without measurement, determining the efficiency and the effectiveness of a new idea is impossible. For example, will the new idea, if implemented, result in an increase in the number of people being served by the organization? If so, by how many? What is this number based on? Once the measure is established, decision makers can ask whether the impact justifies the cost. That is, is the organization getting enough bang for its buck? Or is the buck better invested in another idea?

Objective measures established in the feasibility stage also support ongoing learning about how the organization's actions affect the community when the idea is implemented. Organizations have a clear basis for improvement when they measure actual performance against management's expectations. For example, the management of a human service agency reasons from the experience of other agencies that a new program will bring in 100 new clients. When it is implemented, however, 125 new clients show up. The difference in the assumed and measured impact provides an opportunity for learning about community needs, and this in turn enables the organization to better meet those needs.

Questions to Ask to Assess Impact

☑ What is the specific positive change that the innovation will bring about? The level of impact should also be set as a specific goal or target that management believes is realistic and achievable.

☑ How will that impact be measured? Establish indicators, and provide a means of monitoring them. Set a target number within a specific time frame, and this will be the baseline for success. The monitoring process should be consistent with any existing review and evaluation processes.

The more clearly defined and precise the measures are, the higher the decision makers' scores will be.

Appropriate Scope

Some new ideas exceed the organization's management and resource capacity. The magnitude of the innovation must be taken into account to determine whether the nonprofit has the experience, infrastructure, or resource base to undertake and sustain it. Many good ideas can overwhelm an organization and pose a significant risk of failure if scope is not addressed. The earlier discussion of small organizations that undertake large capital projects is an example of how the scope of a change can refocus staff energy to the detriment of programming in the short run and financial health in the long run. Review of the earlier criteria—in particular, discussions of reasonable cost and fit—provides a basis for understanding whether the scope of the proposed change is appropriate.

Question to Ask to Assess Scope

☑ Are the resources budgeted for the proposed innovation disproportionate to the operating budget of the organization? As a suggested rule of thumb, a project budget in excess of 10 percent of an organization's operating budget is too large to be implemented and managed without causing significant strain on the organization's operations and resources.

The greater the amount budgeted to support the new idea relative to the existing budget, the riskier the innovation is and the lower the decision makers' scores will be.

Personnel

The issue of personnel has already been addressed in part in assessing expertise, cost, and fit. Specific skill sets needed to implement and manage an innovation are critical to its success. Sometimes existing staff members have the appropriate knowledge, experience, and professional skills to support the new activity, but they may already be working at capacity. If they are required to devote time to the new idea, and especially if they are asked to play a major role, existing job responsibilities must be redistributed. The question then arises as to whether the organization has the right staff to take on these reassigned tasks.

If additional personnel must be hired to bring about the change, what are the required skills and the appropriate level of compensation? Specific job descriptions and terms of employment must be developed. Availability is another important consideration. Can people be recruited easily within the local labor market? If not, what are the alternatives and the costs associated with those alternatives?

Questions to Ask to Assess Personnel

- ☑ Does the organization have the appropriate personnel to implement and sustain the proposed new idea? List the specific skill sets they bring to the project. Determine their availability, and, if necessary, assign replacements for their current job responsibilities. If people must be recruited from outside, stipulate their skills sets, write their job descriptions, and determine the costs of recruiting and hiring.

- ☑ Does the organization have the appropriate personnel to manage the innovation? It is critical to manage change carefully, integrating the change with other parts of the organization's operations and negotiating relations with external stakeholders. Take into account not only the personnel needed to implement the change but also the effort of administering and monitoring the change.

The better the decision makers' understanding is of who will staff the project and its impact on the overall staffing of the organization, the better they can score this criterion. The greater the availability of qualified personnel, the higher the score will be.

Practicality

Even if a new idea might be feasible, it might not be practical. In addressing feasibility, the decision makers ask whether something can be done. In addressing practicality, they ask whether it is sensible or useful to do it. Even if an idea is feasible, there may be strong reasons that it is not practical: another organization in the community might be pursuing a similar project, or funding might be limited, or the organization might be considering other new ideas that are more beneficial.

Discussions of practicality are in many ways the most difficult in the feasibility stage, because the decision makers must move from conceptualizing the change to addressing the consequences of implementation.

Question to Ask to Assess Practicality

☑ Should we undertake this new activity at this time? In answering the question, revisit the elements of strategic fit, demonstrated feasibility, human resource requirements, cost, and impact on the organization and community. Weigh the timing of the decision and its potential conflict with other demands on the organization.

If the decision makers find a high degree of fit with the previous criteria as well as a lack of conflict or competing activities, the score on practicality will be high.

Measurable Productivity

Ideally an innovation should result in increased efficiencies in addition to the desired impact or effectiveness. The new activity should enable the organization to do more with existing or acquired resources than it is currently able to do. Productivity, like impact, is a measure of leverage: being able to do more with the resources available.

The assessment of productivity requires objective measures. Simply defined, productivity is measured by dividing the results obtained by the resources expended. For example, if a new process enables program staff to address the needs of twice as many clients, there is a twofold increase in productivity.

Questions to Ask to Assess Productivity

☑ Will successful implementation of the proposed idea have a measurable impact on the productivity of the organization? If so, the positive or negative impact should be defined in a measurable way. In some cases, considerable resources are expended at the early stage of a project but are no longer needed at later stages, so take into account any differences in productivity increase and gains during the course of the activity.

☑ Will increased productivity in one area be offset by a decrease in productivity in another area? For instance, new computer software might provide program staff with a better way to record certain kinds of information, but the effort required from the technical staff to maintain the system and provide ongoing training might offset the gains.

The greater the anticipated increase in measurable productivity, the greater the decision makers' scores will be.

Risk Factors

When a new idea is introduced, there is often a tendency to stress its potential benefits so much that its risks are overshadowed. Decision makers have to resist this tendency and speculate about what can go wrong. This is necessary to assess how well equipped the organization is to correct problems as they come up.

Damage to the organization and community might occur in several ways. Internal risks include (1) technological risk—the loss of the benefits of a piece of equipment or process if it is not adequately managed or supported or simply does not work; (2) personnel risk—what happens if the staff does not possess the necessary skill sets or the organization loses a critical staff member during implementation; and (3) the risk of inadequate funding—when there is not enough money to fully initiate or implement the change.

The greatest external risk is that the change might damage relationships with clients or audience or with funders—(4) market risk.

Question to Ask to Assess Risk Factors

☑ What factors might prevent the successful implementation of the new idea? Pay specific attention to technological, personnel, funding, and market risks. The decision maker should entertain a range of what-if scenarios in each area and determine the most likely organizational response to the damage. If adequate safeguards are in place, the risks can be managed.

The fewer the potential risks and the better the organization is able to manage them if they do occur, the higher the decision makers' scores will be.

Collaboration

The nonprofit sector values collaborative efforts among organizations. They foster a sense of community, provide the opportunity to combine limited resources, and promote learning and organizational improvement. An innovation can benefit more than one organization if several organizations share in its development and implementation.

Questions to Ask to Assess Collaboration

☑ Can more than one organization use the proposed concept effectively? If so, identify the potential collaborators and assess the benefits. This might be accomplished through discussions with potential partners, as well as reviews of their current and planned operations and programming.

☑ How can organizations best pool resources to optimize the benefits of the innovation? This requires advanced planning for how the organizations will work together to initiate and implement the proposed new activity. Consider the roles, responsibilities, resources, and anticipated outcomes for each partner.

The greater the number of viable collaborators and the better developed the goals and plans for working together, the higher the decision makers' scores will be.

Broader Benefit

This factor is similar to collaboration in that it addresses the range of organizations that might ultimately benefit from the new idea once it has been successfully implemented. If an organization fully implements a new program or process, it might be viable and productive in other organizational settings. The innovation can be diffused to a broader group.

Questions to Ask to Assess Broader Benefit

☑ If the innovation is successfully implemented, do its benefits extend beyond the nonprofits that are directly involved? As with collaboration, articulate the benefits in detail, and identify and research the organizations that will profit.

☑ How will the information about the innovation be disseminated? Develop detailed plans for circulating information.

The greater the number of organizations identified that might benefit and the more specific the dissemination plans, the higher the decision makers' scores will be.

Financial Health

Ideally an innovation should enhance the financial health of the organization. That is, it should support the organization's long-term ability to generate revenue, earned and unearned. Some innovations produce revenue streams. While many programs will always require some form of subsidy, if they are clearly developed and demonstrably effective, they are more likely to receive ongoing funding. Often organizations assume a short-term financial risk or burden to initiate an idea on the assumption that it will become self-supporting over time.

Question to Ask to Assess Financial Health

☑ How will the successful implementation of the project contribute to the short- and long-term financial health of the organization? This question is best answered by modeling the costs and revenues associated with the innovation over time.

The greater the short- and long-term benefits of the innovation, the higher the decision makers' scores will be.

Organization Development

In addition to contributing to an organization's overall financial health, a good decision will support its future growth and development in other ways. An innovation can position an organization to do more and better work in the future.

Decision makers should assess the new idea's potential contribution to developing the organization.

Question to Ask to Assess Organization Development

☑ How will the successful implementation of the new idea contribute to the development of the organization in the following areas: (1) staff, both personally and professionally, (2) programming, and (3) administration? Ideally, the decision should increase the staff's skill sets as well as meet their personal and professional goals. It will be a significant problem if the innovation is at odds with their goals. If the innovation is tied to programming, it should enhance the organization's existing and planned activities by increasing content, quality, or reach. Finally, if the change is administrative, it should have the potential for making the organization's work processes more efficient and effective.

The greater the new idea's contribution to staff, program, and administrative development, the higher the decision makers' scores will be.

Board Oversight

This final factor brings the feasibility process full circle. In particular, it ties the decision back to strategic alignment issues through board oversight processes. This is a check on how policies set at the board level address what is being proposed, as well as how existing board review processes would monitor it.

Questions to Ask to Assess Board Oversight

☑ Does the board have the appropriate structures, processes, and policies in place to oversee the decision? The way existing board policies apply to the decision and how monitoring it fits with ongoing board committee work should provide the answers.

☑ Are board members directly involved in the development of what is being proposed, and does this complement or conflict with their board oversight roles? A board member who is championing a new idea might have difficulty maintaining objectivity about the potential risks and rewards. In such cases, appropriate checks and balances should be developed.

The more closely matched with existing board oversight mechanisms and the more clearly defined the board members' involvement, the higher the decision makers' scores will be.

In reviewing the criteria and completing the matrix, decision makers learn more about the idea and potential consequences for the organization. At the end of the process, they should have a well-reasoned opinion whether a new idea is feasible and why. Moreover, they will have collected and organized sufficient information to support their decision and communicate it to the appropriate individuals and groups.

The two minicases that follow illustrate how the feasibility matrix can be used to illustrate the underlying logic in each decision. These cases and the ones in later chapters are based on experiences we have had working with nonprofits. To some of our readers, these minicases might seem simple or far-fetched. But trust us: we can't make this stuff up.

THE CASE OF THE GOTHAM PERFORMING ARTS ALLIANCE

The excellence of a gift lies in its appropriateness rather than in its value.
—*Charles Dudley Warner*

The Gotham Performing Arts Alliance is a small service organization that provides limited support for nonprofit theaters, dance troupes, and musical groups in a small city. It serves its constituents primarily through informational resources such as Web-based directories, a newsletter, and a calendar of events. The alliance also plays a professional development role in the community by hosting master classes and workshops.

The organization has an annual budget of $220,000 and a staff consisting of an executive director, a program director, and a part-time administrative assistant. It is housed in a modest suite of offices in the city's performing arts district.

One day, the executive director, Ms. Smiley, learns of a windfall bequest from one of the alliance's founding board members, a noted patron of the arts in the city, who has passed away and left the organization his residence, a twenty-five-room Victorian mansion. His will stipulates that the alliance must use the house as its headquarters; it cannot sell the property. Furthermore, there is no provision to support operations; the alliance will have to raise the funds to maintain and run the building.

The performing arts community is excited about the possibility of having a permanent home. The board, however, is conflicted: several board members knew the donor personally and feel an obligation to honor his wishes, while others are concerned about the alliance's ability to take on the property. The board chair asks Ms. Smiley to assess the feasibility of accepting the house and moving the alliance. She is to present her findings and recommendations at a special meeting of the board.

Ms. Smiley uses the due diligence process and feasibility matrix. She assigns weights to reflect the board's concerns about the alliance's capacity to take on the bequest. As a result, the most heavily weighted criteria are strategic alignment, reasonable cost, appropriate scope, risk factors, and financial health. Her opinions about each of the criteria are listed below, along with supporting information. Scores are prepared for each and summarized in the matrix in Exhibit 5.2.

Strategic alignment. The alliance supports local theater, dance, and music largely through informational resources. Having a large building to house groups and programming would serve the community, but it is not in keeping with the alliance's strategy. Becoming a landlord would dramatically change the organization's role in the community. Score: 2.

Feasibility. There are several similar service organizations in other cities. All have very small operating budgets and staff complements, and they are housed in rented office space. None has ever considered owning its own space, and none has been offered real estate as part of a gift. Score: 0.

Expertise. No one on the alliance's staff knows anything about converting a house to institutional use or managing and maintaining it. Additional building professionals

Exhibit 5.2. Summary of Ms. Smiley's Scores.

Criteria	Weight	Score	Weighted Score
Strategic alignment	12	2	24
Feasibility	5	0	0
Expertise	3	0	0
Reasonable cost	12	0	0
Fit	3	3	9
Measurable impact	3	2	6
Appropriate scope	12	0	0
Personnel	3	2	6
Practicality	10	0	0
Measurable productivity	3	0	0
Risk factors	12	0	0
Collaboration	3	0	0
Broader benefit	2	8	16
Financial health	12	0	0
Organization development	2	7	14
Board oversight	3	2	6
Totals	**100**	**26**	**81**
Total possible weighted score			**1,000**
Percentage agreement			**8%**

would most likely have to be hired on a consulting basis for the conversion and additional staff recruited to manage the space. Score: 0.

Reasonable cost. Ms. Smiley enlisted a volunteer architect and structural engineer to help estimate the financial resources required to adapt the home and run the facility. An inspection revealed considerable deferred maintenance and that the roof, heating, and electrical systems needed to be replaced. In addition, a number of changes would have to be made to bring the building into line with local building codes for public use. A conservative estimate was that the renovations to the building would cost $3 million and approximately $250,000 annually to maintain the building and grounds. Score: 0.

Fit. The only fit that Ms. Smiley sees with the alliance's current operations is that some of the house could be used for office and program space. But the property is in a neighborhood several miles from the performing arts district and would not be convenient for most of the alliance's constituents. Members of the community see the potential for much-needed office, program, and even performance space that could be available on a rental basis, and they have made their opinions known to the executive director. Score: 3.

Measurable impact. The only positive impact that Ms. Smiley can determine with any certainty is that there would be more available space for the alliance and the performing arts community. How appropriate or accessible that space might be was not determined. Score: 2.

Appropriate scope. The project would require a capital campaign fifteen to twenty times the size of the alliance's operating budget. Once the new building was operational, the budget would have to be at least tripled to support the building and take on the additional staff required to run it. Score: 0.

Personnel. No one currently on staff is able to carry out the project given current workloads. The alliance has never undertaken a large capital project or managed a facility. It is conceivable that appropriate staff could be hired locally, but the alliance does not have the funds in its budget to support the additional personnel. Score: 2.

Practicality. Ms. Smiley feels strongly that accepting the building would undermine the alliance's programming and distort its role in the community. Score: 0.

Measurable productivity. Taking on the overhead associated with a large house in need of extensive repairs would actually decrease the alliance's productivity. It would take significantly more resources to get the same work done. Score: 0.

Risk factors. By the time Ms. Smiley starts to evaluate risk, she can see practically nothing else. There is technological risk: new systems would have to be implemented throughout the mansion. There is personnel risk: the staff people have told her that if the alliance accepts the property, they would leave, and three board members have told her in confidence that they would resign. The financial risk is the most overwhelming risk factor. The little city of Gotham provides few local sources of capital and operating funds. It is likely that the alliance would not be able to raise enough money to make the house a workable space. And there is market risk because of role confusion in the community about who should benefit from the property. Score: 0.

Collaboration. Local performing arts organizations are interested in renting space in the future. None, however, are interested in collaborating to plan and raise the needed capital funds for the mansion. Score: 0.

Broader benefit. If the mansion were converted and space were made available to the nonprofit arts community, the community would indeed benefit. Score: 8.

Financial health. Acquiring the property would put the alliance in an untenable financial position and threaten the organization's viability. Score: 0.

Organization development. The space provides a setting for a large number of possible new programs and relationships within the performing arts community. The mansion would position the organization to develop programming and support the community in new and exciting ways. Score: 7.

Board oversight. The board would have to develop the capacity to oversee a large physical plant. This would mean recruiting board members with the appropriate expertise because the current board has no experience with buildings or capital projects. The board structure would have to be revisited. Issues such as liability and insurance would have to be addressed. Score: 2.

Ms. Smiley's assessment yields a very low percentage of agreement with the criteria: 8 percent. This makes accepting the bequest an extremely risky decision. Ms. Smiley recommends against it.

THE CASE OF THE COMMUNITY RECREATION CENTER

The first rule of tinkering is to save all the parts.
—Paul Erhlich

The Community Recreation Center is a neighborhood institution. Located in a commuter suburb of a major city, it has played a significant role in enhancing the quality of life of its members for the past fifty years. The center houses a wellness center, gymnasiums, a swimming pool, offices, classrooms, meeting rooms, and multipurpose spaces. It offers a variety of programming, including fitness classes for adults, activities for senior citizens, a day care center, a youth swimming program, and special events for families.

The center has always been financially healthy. With an annual operating budget of $6.2 million, it is supported by a diverse mix of funding streams: membership and program fees, government contracts, foundation and corporate grants, and individual donations. To commemorate its fiftieth anniversary, a member has given the center an unrestricted gift of fifty thousand dollars. At the most recent board meeting, the center's executive director, Mr. Thomas, was charged with recommending how the gift should be used.

Mr. Thomas realizes that the gift can easily be spent in a number of ways, such as adding it to the center's endowment or next year's operating budget. However, because the gift is unrestricted, he sees it as an opportunity to explore and develop new program areas. The board's very active three-person program committee works in both oversight and advisory roles, so he discusses his initial thoughts with them and asks them to be part of the decision-making process. Excited by the thought of developing new programming, they agree and meet to discuss how the funds might be best used.

Mr. Thomas and the committee feel that the donation provides a great opportunity, but what kind of programming would be the best to fund? It is clear from the board perspective that any programming must advance the center's mission of enhancing the quality of life of the local community. However, the group is stuck when it comes to recommending specific activities. At this point in the meeting, Mr. Thomas points out that his staff is always coming to him with ideas for new programs, and this might be an opportunity to harness their ideas and enthusiasm. The committee members agree, but they are concerned that the process they use for selecting the program designs be clear to the staff members. Fortunately, Mr. Thomas is familiar with the due diligence process and the matrix tool. He describes these to the committee as a possible approach. They like the method, decide to use it, and schedule another meeting to assign weights to the feasibility matrix and develop guidelines for staff proposals.

The weighting system that the group subsequently develops reflects the importance of fit with mission and the goals that the new programming be a logical complement to what the organization is already doing in the community and be sustainable in the long term. For this reason, the most heavily weighted criteria are strategic alignment, expertise, fit, and organization development. The weights assigned, along with the rationale for each, are presented in Exhibit 5.3.

Mr. Thomas calls a meeting of his senior staff and asks for new program proposals. He is very clear that anything suggested has to meet the due diligence criteria, which he carefully explains to them. As a result, four feasibility proposals are submitted:

Proposal 1, from the director of senior activities: Develop a nutrition education program for seniors with the assistance of a consultant. Cost over three years: $30,000.

Proposal 2, from the director of the day care center: Work with a local college nutrition institute to put in place an internship program that will develop, introduce, staff, and evaluate healthy eating programming in the day care center. Cost over three years: $18,000.

Exhibit 5.3. Community Recreation Center Weighted Feasibility Matrix with Rationale and Comments.

Criteria	Weight	Rationale/Comments
Strategic alignment	14	Previously projects have been proposed outside the mission
Feasibility	5	Good ideas successfully implemented elsewhere are appropriate
Expertise	12	Quality programming is dependent on those developing it

(Continued)

Exhibit 5.3. *(Continued)*		
Criteria	*Weight*	*Rationale/Comments*
Reasonable cost	8	Realistic budgets are necessary
Fit	12	Must fit with existing programming and community needs
Measurable impact	5	Must make measurable improvement in quality of life
Appropriate scope	5	Must be reasonable in terms of department budgets
Personnel	5	Staff tends to be overly ambitious and takes on too much
Practicality	2	Must complement operating plans and current budgets
Measurable productivity	2	This is not a key concern
Risk factors	5	Must consider long-term market (community) and financial risk
Collaboration	2	Collaborative projects are good but not necessary
Broader benefit	2	Dissemination is not critical at this stage
Financial health	4	Long-term financial impact should be addressed
Organization development	12	Must enhance capacity of center in the long term
Board oversight	5	Should fit with policies and work of board program committee
Total	**100**	

Proposal 3, from the director of the wellness center: Develop a weight-control program for wellness center members. Cost over three years: $36,000.

Proposal 4, from the director of facilities: Develop a plan for advertising and renting out unused center space to other community organizations. Cost for one year: $2,200.

The board program committee members along with Mr. Thomas score all the proposals. Proposals 1, 2, and 3 all score highly. There is some question about whether proposal 4 meets the requirements. A summary of the percentage agreement for each based on the committee along with Mr. Thomas's scores is presented in Table 5.1.

Based on the scoring and the available funds, the committee could recommend that proposals 1 and 2 be funded. However, in closely reviewing the proposals, it became clear that nutrition and obesity are an overarching theme of the first three. Clearly, these are national public health issues that greatly affect quality of life and health in the local community. Currently none of the center's programming addresses these issues. After some discussion, the committee and Mr. Thomas agree that the $50,000 can be best spent developing an integrated program plan that addresses healthy eating.

Mr. Thomas goes back to the staff with his findings. Although the directors who submitted the proposals are at first disappointed that their projects will not be funded, they quickly see the value of working together on the bigger project. The center's director of development is at the meeting, and she becomes engaged as well. She knows of several current foundation initiatives that will support programs to address nutrition and obesity issues. If the program directors rework their ideas into a more comprehensive

Table 5.1. Percentage Agreement for Initial Proposals, Community Recreation Center.

Proposal	Committee Member 1	Committee Member 2	Committee Member 3	Mr. Thomas	Average % Agreement
Proposal 1	93%	82%	87%	90%	88%
Proposal 2	90	80	88	86	86
Proposal 3	87	79	70	80	79
Proposal 4	65	30	22	44	40

proposal, the $50,000 committed to the project internally can be used to leverage external initiative funding.

The staff works together to produce a comprehensive proposal. The director of facilities even develops a scheme to allocate excess building capacity to the healthy eating programming and initiates discussions with a commercial weight-loss group about renting classroom space. The cost of this program is covered by many of the center members' health plans, so that while providing income, it will also be aligned with the center's mission.

Before presenting the proposal for integrated programming to the board committee, Mr. Thomas reviews it using the feasibility matrix. His findings and rationale are presented in Exhibit 5.4.

With agreement at 86 percent, Mr. Thomas deems it a feasible proposal. Two areas of concern, staffing and long-term sustainability, will have to be monitored and actively managed. Because of the committee's familiarity with the matrix, they quickly see and understand the proposal's strengths and the areas that will require ongoing attention. They agree with Mr. Thomas's assessment and support his decision that the staff move forward and develop the healthy eating programming.

The Community Recreation Center provides an example of how the due diligence process and feasibility matrix can be used by groups to learn about the organization and build consensus. Based on the first round of matrix analysis carried out with the board committee, Mr. Thomas could have decided to fund two of the initial proposals with a reasonable expectation of success, even if they were limited in scope. But by using the process and matrix as tools to fully study, understand, and communicate how all the pieces of programming fit together, the board and staff were able to tinker with the ideas. The result was a much better decision.

Exhibit 5.4. Mr. Thomas's Evaluation of the Integrated Healthy Eating Proposal.

Criteria	Weight	Mr. Thomas's Score	Weighted Score	Rationale
Strategic alignment	14	10	140	Excellent alignment with quality-of-life mission
Feasibility	5	8	40	Realistic programs; some have succeeded elsewhere
Expertise	12	7	84	Will require new skills and consultants
Reasonable cost	8	9	72	Detailed realistic budgets have been developed
Fit	12	9	108	Complements existing programs
Measurable impact	5	10	50	Reliable measures exist to assess impact
Appropriate scope	5	9	45	What is proposed is phased, not overly ambitious
Personnel	5	7	35	Staff will require additional training/support
Practicality	2	9	18	Issue is pressing, and resources are available
Measurable productivity	2	6	12	Some productivity gains through shared resources
Risk factors	5	8	40	New funding streams needed to sustain effort
Collaboration	2	7	14	Some collaborative programming
Broader benefit	2	6	12	Structured so results can be disseminated
Financial health	4	7	28	Current funding priority but long-term concerns
Organization development	12	10	120	Will enhance center's overall capabilities
Board oversight	5	9	45	Aligned with work of board program committee
Totals	**100**	**131**	**863**	
Total possible weighted score			**1,000**	
Percentage agreement			**86%**	

6

Stage Two: Pilot

Nature herself has never attempted to effect great changes rapidly.

—Quintilian

PILOTING A NEW IDEA is the first careful step in making a critical decision real. It provides a way of testing a feasible concept further by putting it into practice in a limited and controlled way. In the pilot stage of due diligence, the risks and benefits of the idea emerge and can be compared to those anticipated in the feasibility assessment. By treating the pilot as an experiment, the decision makers can evaluate the actual impact on the organization. Management is able to contain and limit the damage of an idea that might have looked great on paper but failed to yield the anticipated results in application. And if the idea meets or exceeds expectations, the pilot provides an opportunity to modify and enhance it prior to full implementation.

This chapter begins with a discussion of what to consider in moving from concept to action. The process encompasses taking a well-developed idea to a messy and complex reality, where there are almost always unanticipated consequences. We stress the importance of treating the pilot as a project, limited by a clearly defined scope and time frame. Once the project is designed, the organization is ready to enter the second stage of due diligence: deciding whether to pilot the idea. We then present the matrix for supporting the pilot decision and include all the due diligence criteria, as we did in Chapter Five. Once again, being as thorough as possible at this early stage smoothes the progress toward full implementation. The guiding questions for each of the criteria are slightly different from those set out in the feasibility stage, and the weightings that the decision makers assign will most likely be different also. The chapter concludes with two minicases illustrating how pilot decisions can be made using the matrix.

Piloting the Feasible Decision

Knowledge must come through action; you can have no test which is not fanciful save by trial.

—Sophocles

Once a new concept has been judged feasible, the next step is to determine whether it is appropriate for the organization to implement. Ideas that are feasible might not be practical. Because something can be done does not mean that it necessarily should be done. The primary purpose of the pilot decision is to determine whether a feasible idea is practical, answering the question, "Should our organization do this?"

In assessing whether a feasible idea is practical, the decision makers should address exactly how they can carefully approach putting the concept into action. Instead of moving to full implementation, testing the idea in a limited way can determine what the impact will be for a particular organization in its specific context. Even if an idea has been successfully implemented many times by similar groups, there might be conditions that would prevent the organization now considering the idea from putting it into practice. In determining whether to test an idea, the decision makers should design the pilot in such a way that they will answer the key questions related to risk, leverage, and sustainability.

In making a feasibility decision, the decision makers carefully assess available information about whether the idea has succeeded or failed in other organizations to determine whether the new idea might work for their specific situation. As we saw in Chapter Four, if an idea is judged feasible, the decision makers feel that it has a reasonable chance at success. At that stage, however, the idea remains promising but unproven. To commit resources to fully implementing the idea, the decision makers should also have some demonstrated and documented success with application.

In deciding whether to move forward, the decision makers should revisit the idea with the focus on what will be required to take action. First, they should review the due diligence criteria from a narrower perspective: that of their organization at the specific point in time when they will put the idea into practice. This enables them to examine their situation in greater detail, collecting more organization-specific information. Also, in many cases, significant time will have passed between the feasibility study and the pilot. Changes in the nonprofit world can happen very quickly, and new information may have significant impact on the decision to test the idea.

Second, the decision makers must address the design of an appropriate pilot. That is, they must determine exactly what resources will be used, which parts of the organization will be involved, over what time period, and what the specific intended outcomes will be. By treating the pilot as a discrete project with a beginning, middle, and end, the decision makers test the new idea while containing the risk.

In many ways, the decision to pilot the idea is the most difficult phase in the due diligence process. This is the point where the organization, its resources, and its relationship with the community are put at risk. The decision makers bear the responsibility for making a judgment that can result in success or failure. If a new idea is demonstrated to be feasible, its seductive quality can actually be amplified, for it has been thoroughly investigated and deemed possible. The decision makers should therefore approach the pilot cautiously and with what we like to call brutal honesty, challenging their assumptions about the benefits of proceeding.

Deciding not to go forward with the pilot is a viable option. An idea that has worked elsewhere might be too risky or provide too little return on the amount of time and energy invested. Or the situation may have changed since the time it was proposed, and the concept has become obsolete.

Designing the Pilot Project

Luck is the residue of design.
—Branch Rickey

In designing the pilot, the decision makers should develop a test that will provide the maximum amount of information with the least amount of risk to the organization. Putting limits on a good idea works against the momentum generated by a successful feasibility assessment; nonetheless, a deliberate and conservative pilot is the most responsible way to proceed. If a new idea successfully tests out in the pilot phase, the organization can move to full implementation with confidence. If the time and effort are devoted to a careful test that realistically addresses the promise and the problems associated with the new idea, success is the result of well-developed and informed process, not luck.

The pilot should be viewed as a project with a distinct beginning, middle, and end. The purpose of the project is to test the innovation in a limited way. Setting the limits on the pilot is critical for managing risk, understanding if the anticipated leverage can be realized, and determining exactly what resources will be needed if full implementation is indicated.

In assessing the pilot, the decision makers work from a project plan. The plan is usually a team effort by those who proposed the original idea and those who will eventually implement it. Sometimes individuals with additional expertise are also involved. For example, testing a new computer system originally championed by the information technology department should also tap end users and perhaps external hardware and software consultants for the team.

The project should be limited in scope and duration. Scope reflects the amount of resources the organization wishes to risk and the level of activity needed to provide meaningful results about the pilot's success or failure. The duration of the pilot—the time it takes to implement and monitor it and assess the results—should also be set. Some projects can be tested relatively quickly, within weeks, and others require many months. It is not unusual for major innovations to be piloted over the course of a year in order to determine the effects of the annual cycle of regular organizational activity.

As with any other project, a pilot budget, fully detailing the costs, should also be developed. A close analysis of the resources required and the available funding sources provides an opportunity for learning about the level of investment required to bring about the change. Comparing the amount budgeted with the intended internal and external impact provides a better idea of what the leverage will be.

A detailed evaluation plan with specific requirements for success and failure should be established. The initial assumptions about the measurable impact of the project provide a baseline for evaluating its actual results. The expected outcomes of the pilot should be made explicit and measurable. The appropriate individuals should be responsible for monitoring progress and collecting and analyzing the necessary data as the project unfolds. This assessment will provide the objective information ultimately used to determine whether the organization should move to full implementation at the conclusion of the pilot.

The Pilot Matrix

There's a difference between knowing the Path and walking the Path.

—*Andy and Larry Wachowski,* **The Matrix**

The pilot matrix, like the feasibility matrix in the previous chapter, is based on the model in Chapter Four. The matrix in Exhibit 6.1 incorporates all the due diligence criteria from Chapter Three and allows any number of decision makers to assess the pilot with a weighted scoring system. Criteria are identical to those for the feasibility matrix. However, the questions asked for each due diligence criterion are slightly different from those in the feasibility stage. Here, they guide the assessment of the proposed pilot and lay the groundwork for future implementation if the pilot is successful. The emphasis in this stage is on taking action given the organization's current resources, operations, and environment. As we will see in the minicases, the weighting of each question is often shifted to reflect this new emphasis. As with the feasibility matrix, the more heavily weighted the criteria are, the more important they are to minimizing risk, maximizing leverage, and ensuring sustainability of the outcome.

Exhibit 6.1. Sample Individual Pilot Matrix.

Criteria	Weight	Decision Maker Score	Weighted Score
Strategic alignment			
Feasibility			
Expertise			
Reasonable cost			
Fit			
Measurable impact			
Appropriate scope			
Personnel			
Practicality			
Measurable productivity			
Risk factors			
Collaboration			
Broader benefit			
Financial health			
Organization development			
Board oversight			
Totals	**100**		
Total possible weighted score			**1,000**
Percentage agreement			**%**

A set of questions for each of the criteria that guide the decision makers in scoring follows. As with the questions related to the feasibility criteria, if a decision maker can answer them precisely with the specific information required, a higher score will result. If the decision maker cannot answer precisely or if the answers do not support the decision criteria, the score will be lower.

Strategic Alignment

In assessing feasibility, decision makers evaluate how the proposed idea fits within the general strategy of the organization. Pilot activities are closely reviewed and compared with the detailed goals and action steps that make up an organization's strategic plan. It should be clear how the pilot will fit within the organization's vision, mission, objectives, and goals, as well as how it will improve the organization's ability to pursue its priorities. In some situations, the idea that is originally proposed turns out to be a better fit on the conceptual and philosophical level than it is on the practical level. It's in the design of the pilot that problems with strategic fit tied to implementation begin to arise.

Questions to Ask to Assess Strategic Alignment

- ☑ How does this pilot project fit within the organization's existing strategic and operating plans? Which goals and activities does it support? How specifically will it support them?

- ☑ What is the potential strategic impact of the pilot project? That is, does it significantly improve the organization's ability to pursue major high-priority action items that will have a large effect on the organization overall? How will it do so? Or will it only marginally contribute to minor low-priority items that affect only specific programs or departments?

Once the decision makers understand in detail how the pilot will specifically support the organization's strategy, they assign a score. The better defined the fit and the greater the anticipated positive impact on advancing the strategy are, the higher the score will be.

Feasibility

At the pilot stage, some new ideas have already been successfully implemented and have been demonstrated to be possible. In other cases, where the idea has never been tried before, the benefits of implementation versus the risks have been thoroughly examined through what-if scenarios, and the idea deemed feasible in principle.

In making the decision to pilot the new idea, the feasibility of implementation requires close scrutiny. In the case of ideas successfully demonstrated elsewhere, the decision makers should carefully examine the other situations where the idea was implemented to understand the similarities and differences. If the new idea has been judged feasible in principle, assumptions about the organization and context that led to that conclusion must be compared with how the organization actually works in the community.

There is a greater likelihood of success if an idea has already been implemented successfully by similar organizations under similar conditions. And the more widespread the idea is in practice, the greater the chance is that it will work in another organization.

The decision makers must research the proposed innovation to determine if and how it has worked in other settings.

Questions to Ask to Assess Feasibility

☑ What are the specific similarities and differences between this non-profit and the organization that successfully implemented the idea? The more similar they are, the more likely the pilot is to succeed.

☑ Given appropriate financial and human resources, can the project be implemented? Here the designers of the pilot begin to detail the appropriate human and financial resources and how they will ensure that the pilot is a success.

The more evidence there is showing that the idea has worked in similar situations in other organizations and the better the understanding is of the resources required, the higher the decision makers' scores will be.

Practicality

A new idea might be feasible but not practical. The practicality of the idea becomes more important as the organization considers implementation. Even if it is possible to pilot the concept, perhaps there are strong reasons that it is not sensible or useful for the organization to pursue it, or to pursue it at this time.

Question to Ask to Assess Practicality

☑ Should the concept be piloted at this time—or at all? In answering this question, the decision makers should revisit strategic alignment and how the pilot will advance the organization's purpose. They should also review the resources required with the anticipated results of the pilot project to determine if anything has changed internally or externally that could affect them. Finally, if timing is an issue, they should determine if it makes sense to postpone the pilot to a later date.

The greater chances for success are at the time of the pilot, the higher the decision makers' scores will be.

Expertise

The pilot will most likely involve the introduction of new knowledge into the organization. Indeed, a considerable portion of the cost and effort in introducing a new idea can be tied to the expertise necessary to establish a new program or process. It is a major portion of the start-up cost. There is a danger of underestimating the expertise required to pilot an innovation. Although the scope and timing might be abbreviated, this does not necessarily mean that the pilot requires proportionally less expertise. Indeed, in some cases, the pilot might demand a greater level of expertise to initiate something on a limited basis. Assessing the specialized knowledge required for the pilot and how it will be used is necessary to adequately test the new concept.

The pilot plans should clearly stipulate the skill sets and expertise required not only to implement the pilot but to manage it and evaluate it as well. Where this competence will come from and what it will cost should be spelled out in detail.

Questions to Ask to Assess Expertise

☑ What type of specialized knowledge is needed? Describe the programmatic, administrative, or technical skills the pilot needs, and state how they will help implement and evaluate the pilot.

☑ Does the necessary expertise already reside within the organization? If staff members have the demonstrated expertise to implement or assess the pilot, stipulate the scope of their involvement and discuss in detail how their skills sets will be used.

☑ If you have to get expertise from outside the organization, where will it come from? Is it readily available in the local labor market or in existing pools of volunteers? Or will the organization have to go outside the community to obtain it? If the expertise must come from an external source through hiring a temporary staff person or consultant or through volunteer involvement, how will these people be recruited? In your pilot plan, provide specific job descriptions and qualifications, and lay out how you will bring in the appropriate specialists.

☑ If the expertise must be obtained from outside the organization, will there be sufficient transfer of knowledge to the organization during the pilot to move on to full implementation without going outside again? If the pilot is successful, the knowledge should become resident within the organization. The pilot plan should provide a scheme for transferring the knowledge to the current staff, providing additional permanent staff, or maintaining contractual or volunteer arrangements on an ongoing basis.

The better the type of expertise needed is understood, the more available it is, and the more easily it is transferred to the organization, the higher the decision makers' scores will be.

Fit

The pilot will have a short-term effect on the organization both internally and externally. In part, it will provide a preliminary view of how full implementation of the new idea will fit with the nonprofit's ongoing programs and operations. The pilot plan should include the assumptions about its intended positive effects on the organization and community. It should also address any potential negative effects and courses of action for addressing them.

In terms of internal operations, the pilot plan and time line should lay out in detail how to introduce the new activities. Staff assignments, scheduling, and use of space and equipment should be managed to prevent the disruption of existing programs and processes.

The pilot plan should also address the anticipated impact on the broader community: the people served by the nonprofit, other organizations affected by the pilot, and funders.

Questions to Ask to Assess Fit

- ☑ How does the pilot fit within the organization's annual operating plans? If the pilot is to succeed, it should be integrated with ongoing programmatic or administrative work. Determine exactly who will carry out the pilot and how it will affect existing workloads and job assignments. Assess the potential impact of allocating other resources, such as space and equipment, to the pilot. Review the proposed timing of the pilot in terms of the organization's routine activities.

- ☑ How will the pilot affect the community? Answering this question requires an understanding of how the external stakeholders will be involved in the pilot.

The better the fit is with internal operations as well as the interests of external stakeholders, the higher the decision makers' scores will be.

Measurable Impact

The pilot will result in limited changes in programming or operations. A set of specific measurements is required to assess whether the test is effective and to what degree. These measurements should be tied directly to the pilot's goals. Objectively measuring positive impact and any negative consequences is a sound basis for assessing the viability of the project for future full implementation.

Questions to Ask to Assess Impact

☑ What is the specific positive change the pilot is intended to make? Articulating clearly the results sought from the pilot will establish the baseline for measuring success.

☑ How will the pilot's impact be measured? Establish quantitative indicators, and decide how to monitor them. The results will be used to evaluate the impact of the pilot.

The more clearly defined the anticipated changes and the more precise the measures of impact are, the higher the decision makers' scores will be.

Reasonable Cost

A detailed budget with narrative should be developed as part of the pilot plan. The budget should include all the costs associated with the project and demonstrate that there are adequate sources of support. Developing a realistic budget requires careful assessment of personnel requirements, along with space, equipment, and supplies.

Questions to Ask to Assess Cost

☑ What are all the costs associated with the pilot? Develop a budget including direct and indirect costs, fixed and variable costs, and sunk versus relevant future costs. A clearly detailed narrative should accompany the budget detailing the reasoning behind each line item.

☑ Are the budgeted amounts realistic? The decision makers should review the assumptions that lie behind the amounts in each budget line.

☑ Where will the resources in the budget come from? Tie each line item to a reliable source of funds.

The more the decision makers know about the costs and the greater their confidence in the accuracy of the budget and the sources of funds is, the higher their scores will be.

Appropriate Scope

In testing an idea, limited execution of the concept occurs. In the design of the pilot project, implementation is scaled down to limit risk. The process of dividing the project into segments or phases enables the organization to better understand resource requirements and impact on existing programs and operations. If the innovation is broad in scope, the development of the pilot can provide the organization with a way of implementing it in a series of discrete stages to reduce risk further. For example, an organization that wishes to replace its existing computer system can introduce the new system incrementally. That way, the installation of the new system can be tested and refined department by department.

Review of the earlier criteria—in particular, fit and reasonable cost—provides a basis for understanding whether the scope of the pilot itself is appropriate.

Question to Ask to Assess Scope

☑ Are the resources budgeted for the proposed pilot disproportionate to those budgeted for similar activities in the organization? If a pilot project requires a larger budget than other activities do, that should be balanced by its anticipated positive impact. A large investment should result in a large return. The size of the risk the organization is taking should be balanced by the size of the anticipated reward.

The more consistent the pilot budget is with other existing project, program, and department budgets in the organization, the higher the decision makers' scores will be.

Personnel

Developing a pilot plan and budget requires evaluating the strengths and limitations of the current staff. Even if employees have the appropriate knowledge, experience, and professional skills to test the new activity, they might already be fully committed to other projects. Therefore, the pilot plan should include how human resources will be reallocated for the duration of the project. Often staff require extra training or additional support from external consultants. If additional support and personnel are required, plans should be developed for how they will they be recruited, contracted, and compensated.

Question to Ask to Assess Personnel

☑ Does the organization have the appropriate personnel to carry out the pilot? Enumerate the specific skill sets they bring to the project, determine their availability, and work out who will assume their current job responsibilities. If workers must be recruited from the outside, stipulate the skills sets they need, and develop job descriptions and recruitment plans.

The greater the availability of qualified personnel and the ability to allocate personnel to appropriate work during the pilot are, the higher the decision makers' score will be.

Measurable Productivity

The pilot tests the leverage of the new concept. It enables management to measure and assess the benefits gained from the resources invested.

The pilot should result in increased operating efficiency, enabling the organization to do more with the resources it has. The project should be designed in such a way that the anticipated increases in productivity are well defined and data are collected throughout the trial to test these assumptions. At the end of the pilot, the actual result—the measurable impact—is divided by the resources expended, and this provides a measure of productivity.

Questions to Ask to Assess Productivity

☑ Will the pilot have a measurable impact on the productivity of the organization? If so, the positive or negative impact should be defined in a measurable way. Also, in some cases, the start-up costs of initiating the pilot will be significant and skew the results. Make reasonable adjustments in these situations.

☑ Will the pilot increase productivity in one area only to decrease it in another area? Although the end users in our example of implementing a new computer system will be more efficient, the information technology staff might have to take on a new training function that offsets the productivity gains across the organization.

The greater the measurable productivity gains are, the higher the decision makers' scores will be.

Risk Factors

The pilot plan should address what could go wrong during the test, along with contingency plans to manage it. The key areas of risk should be examined: technological, personnel, financial, and market risk.

Question to Ask to Assess Risk

☑ What factors might prevent a successful pilot? The pilot plan should present the potential risk scenarios addressing these factors, along with reasonable strategies to manage any problems.

The more clearly the pilot plan addresses the potential risks associated with the pilot and how they can be managed, the higher the decision makers' scores will be.

Collaboration

If the pilot provides a way to foster collaboration among organizations, the process can strengthen the nonprofit community. Limited resources can be more fully leveraged, and organizational learning and development are promoted. If more than one organization is participating in the pilot, all can share in both the risk and the benefit of the innovation.

Questions to Ask to Assess Collaboration

☑ Does the pilot test the application of the new concept in more than one organization? The pilot plan should address how the test will affect all organizations involved in terms of programming and operations.

☑ How will the organizations pool resources during the pilot? Outline the roles, responsibilities, resources, and anticipated outcomes for each partner.

The greater the number of collaborators and the better developed the goals and plans for working together are, the higher the decision makers' scores will be.

Broader Benefit

Whether a pilot succeeds or fails, other organizations can learn from the experience. If the results are positive, other nonprofits might want to adopt and test similar programming. If the pilot is a failure and the results of the experiment are shared, other nonprofits can avoid its problems. The pilot should enhance learning across the community of nonprofits.

Question to Ask to Assess Broader Benefit

☑ How will the results of the pilot be disseminated? Identify key stakeholders, and develop detailed plans to circulate and discuss the pilot's results.

The greater the number of organizations that can benefit and the more specific the dissemination plans are, the higher the decision makers' scores will be.

Financial Health

The pilot plan should address the financial impact of the innovation. Ideally, even in limited application, a successful test should support the organization's long-term ability to generate revenue, earned and unearned. For example, a pilot program that is successful and yields a measurable benefit to the community might position the organization to develop a better contributed income base.

Question to Ask to Assess Financial Health

☑ How will a successful pilot enhance both the short- and long-term financial health of the organization? This question is best answered by projecting the costs and revenues associated with the pilot. The more precise the understanding of the impact on the organization's financials is, the better the assessment will be.

The greater the financial benefits of the innovation are, the higher the decision makers' scores will be.

Organization Development

The pilot should give clear indications of how the change will support the organization's future growth and development. The test can position the organization to better meet the needs of the community. For example, staff might acquire new skills that help them in program areas beyond the pilot, new client groups might become aware of the organization for the first time, or a partnership with another nonprofit might lead to future collaborations.

Question to Ask to Assess Organization Development

☑ How will the pilot contribute to the development of the organization's program and administrative areas?

The greater the pilot's ability is to contribute to the nonprofit's development in specific ways, the higher the decision makers' scores will be.

Board Oversight

Final approval of the pilot and review of its results should be aligned with board oversight processes. The risks and rewards of implementing a new idea, even in a limited way, should ultimately be subject to formal board review. Whether a pilot program succeeds or fails, the board is ultimately responsible for the consequences. Any board involvement in the pilot process must be carefully planned and structured to avoid any conflicts of role or interest.

Questions to Ask to Assess Board Oversight

☑ How does implementing the pilot and reporting the results fit within the system of board structures, processes, and policies? The project should clearly fit within the work of existing board committees, reflect strategic priorities set by the board, and be governed by organizational policies set by the board.

☑ Are board members directly involved in the pilot? If they are, does this complement or conflict with their board oversight roles? If a board member is directly involved in the pilot, put appropriate checks and balances in place.

The more closely matched with existing board oversight mechanisms and the more clearly defined board member involvement, the higher the decision makers' scores will be.

In assessing the pilot, the decision makers learn the risks of putting an idea into practice and the resources that will be needed. Working through the due diligence criteria with the help of the matrix, they gain a shared understanding of expected outcomes as well as the project's impact on the organization. In doing this work, they will have developed a method for assessing the pilot that will shape the next stage of the critical decision process, moving to full implementation.

The two minicases that follow illustrate how the pilot matrix can be used. In the first, the decision makers are choosing between two similar options. In the second, they are using both the pilot matrix and feasibility matrix to allocate resources across the two categories.

THE CASE OF THE NEIGHBORHOOD FAMILY SERVICE CENTER

We cannot always build the future for our youth,
but we can build our youth for the future.
—Franklin D. Roosevelt

The Neighborhood Family Service Center provides a range of social services to low-income families in a large city. It operates in a converted commercial building located in the geographical heart of the community it serves. Recently the center received a grant to develop additional life skills programming for at-risk youth. Mr. Jones, the director of youth programs, developed two possible programs based on work already done in similar organizations. They are identical in terms of content and staffing, but one is housed at the center and the other at a local high school, where most of the center's teens attend classes. Both are feasible options.

There is enough funding to pilot only one program, so Mr. Jones is faced with selecting which one is a better fit for the center. He and the center's executive director, Ms. Lewis, use the matrix to assess each proposed pilot individually. They develop the weighting jointly, because Mr. Jones understands what it takes to implement a program, while Ms. Lewis has a broader understanding of how any new programs will affect the center's broader operations. Once they have set up the weighted matrix, they decide to review and score each of the criteria separately to avoid influencing one another. Then they meet to compare their scores and arrive at the final decision. A brief description of each proposed program, a summary of the directors' scores, a composite matrix, and a discussion of their final decision follow.

Option 1: Pilot the Life Skills Program at the Center

The program for at-risk youth can be tested on-site at the Neighborhood Family Service Center building.

Strategic alignment. The program is in keeping with a major priority area in the center's strategic plan of developing support for at-risk youth. Jones's score: 10, Lewis's score: 9.

Feasibility. The program was originally developed and implemented successfully in another city ten years ago. Since then, it has been adopted by more than fifty youth service organizations nationwide, and many in the field consider it to be a model program. Jones's score: 10, Lewis's score: 9.

Practicality. Given the emphasis on youth in the center's latest strategic plan, the dedicated group of youth development specialists on staff, and funder support for the pilot, there is strong evidence that the center should carry out the pilot at this time. However, the center building is already at full capacity, and reassigning the space the program requires will be a considerable disruption to current programs. Jones's score: 8, Lewis's score: 7.

Expertise. One of the youth development coordinators on the center's staff participated in the implementation of the same life skills program where she last worked. She would play a major role in setting up, implementing, and assessing the pilot. Jones's score: 10, Lewis's score: 10.

Fit. The youth development staff recently completed another project so now has the time to carry out the pilot. The only internal problem is the one related to available space. The community advisory board that deals with youth issues has been stressing the need for a life skills program for the past three years because there is nothing like it available locally. Moreover, a number of local funders have made supporting children and youth programming a priority. Jones's score: 9, Lewis's score: 8.

Measurable impact. As a result of its application in numerous other cities, there is a set of reliable and valid measures to assess impact. Jones's score: 10, Lewis's score: 10.

Reasonable cost. A detailed budget for the pilot was developed as part of the funding proposal. The center does not have to bear the cost of program development or external staff trainers or evaluators. The primary costs will be those associated with staffing and administrative overhead. Supplies are minimal, and space is fixed. There is a committed funding source for the pilot. Jones's score: 10, Lewis's score: 10.

Appropriate scope. The pilot plan will deliver the one-year program to fifteen participants. If fully implemented, the program would be expanded to multiple cohorts of fifteen in one-year cycles. This would allow the center to test the effectiveness of the complete program with an appropriate number of participants. Jones's score: 10, Lewis's score: 10.

Personnel. This criterion was already addressed in assessing expertise and fit. The current staff have the appropriate skills and the available time to fully implement and evaluate the pilot. Jones's score: 10, Lewis's score: 10.

Measurable productivity. The new program will allow the center to better serve at-risk youth and therefore be more effective in the community. However, it is not clear at this point if and how the life skills programming will increase staff or organizational productivity. Jones's score: 5, Lewis's score: 3.

Risk factors. There are two risk factors. The first is the risk of inadequate space. The second is the risk that the staff member who has had prior experience with the life skills program might leave the center, although she has made a commitment to stay through the pilot. Jones's score: 8, Lewis's score: 7.

Collaboration. Although the youth development director did visit the nonprofit that developed the program to learn about it, the center has not directly collaborated with any local organizations in its implementation. Jones's score: 5, Lewis's score: 2.

Broader benefit. The funder has required that the center develop a plan to disseminate the results of the pilot to the community and other family service agencies regionally. The staff will be circulating a report and providing organizations interested in the program with opportunities to meet and discuss it. Jones's score: 9, Lewis's score: 7.

Financial health. Although the current funding will support only the pilot, several other foundations are interested in supporting implementation on an ongoing basis if the test is successful. Jones's score: 9, Lewis's score: 6.

Organization development. The program will support the development of new skills for the program staff involved in the pilot. Jones's score: 8, Lewis's score: 5.

Board oversight. The center's board is not directly involved in programming decisions. However, the board was instrumental in setting the strategic priorities for the organization and will monitor the results of the pilot as part of its review of progress made against the center's plans. Jones's score: 7, Lewis's score: 8.

Option 2: Pilot the Life Skills Programming at the Local High School

The content, staffing, and timing of the pilot for this option are identical to option 1. The only difference is that the training sessions will be held in an available classroom at the local high school attended by most of the teens in the program. The school is located two blocks from the center.

In reviewing option 2, Jones's and Lewis's assessments and scores remain the same for the following criteria: strategic alignment, feasibility, expertise, measurable impact, reasonable cost, appropriate scope, personnel, risk factors, and organization development. Most of these are related to program content and staffing. However, there are significant differences in the following areas:

Practicality. The high school is offering the use of classroom space at no charge. The life skills program fits well with the school's own priorities of developing after-school programming. Since the only reservations Jones and Lewis had about the practicality of the pilot were based on the limited space at the center, option 2 scores higher than option 1 on this criterion. Jones's score: 10, Lewis's score: 10.

Fit. With option 1, the only concern regarding operational fit was related to reallocating space. With the space issue resolved, this score also increases. Jones's score: 10, Lewis's score: 10.

Measurable productivity. Holding the life skills pilot off-site eliminates overhead costs related to space. Because the center will be committing fewer resources to the program, its productivity will increase. The magnitude of the productivity increase is not large, but it allows the center to maintain operations at current levels. Jones's score: 8, Lewis's score: 5.

Collaboration. Option 2 provides the opportunity to collaborate with another community organization, the high school. Jones's score: 9, Lewis's score: 6.

Broader benefit. The high school has agreed to play a role in disseminating the results of the pilot. It will distribute information on the life skills programming as an after-school program to its network of secondary education institutions. Jones's score: 10, Lewis's score: 8.

Financial health. Housing the program at a public high school opens up additional government funding streams for after-school programming if the pilot is successful. Jones's score: 10, Lewis's score: 7.

Board oversight. One of the center's board members also sits on the board of the school district. Although this relationship does not formally strengthen the oversight processes of the center's board, it does create heightened awareness of and interest in the issues. Jones's score: 8, Lewis's score: 9.

Exhibit 6.2 shows that option 2, with its percentage agreement of 94 percent, is a better choice than option 1, with 88 percent. The scores are relatively close, as one would expect with two similarly good options. It also reflects that Jones's scores are systematically higher than Lewis's. This could be the result of personal style, or it could reflect Jones's investment and belief in the program as its original champion. This is not a major issue in this case, because both decision makers score the second option higher than the first for the same reasons.

THE CASE OF THE INNOVATION FUND

> *One of the serious obstacles to the improvement of our race is indiscriminate charity.*
>
> —*Andrew Carnegie*

Mr. Wheeler is a program officer at a private foundation that awards most of its grants to local nonprofits in the areas of human services, arts and culture, health care, and the

Exhibit 6.2. Summary of Mr. Jones's and Ms. Lewis's Scores.

Criteria	Weight	Jones, Option 1	Lewis, Option 1	Option 1 Total Weighted Score	Jones, Option 2	Lewis, Option 2	Option 2 Total Weighted Score
Strategic alignment	15	10	9	285	10	9	285
Feasibility	12	10	9	228	10	9	228
Practicality	12	8	7	180	10	10	240
Expertise	10	10	10	200	10	10	200
Fit	10	9	8	170	10	10	200
Measurable impact	10	10	10	200	10	10	200
Reasonable cost	5	10	10	100	10	10	100
Appropriate scope	5	10	10	100	10	10	100
Personnel	4	10	10	80	10	10	80
Measurable productivity	4	5	3	32	8	5	52
Risk factors	4	8	7	60	8	7	60
Collaboration	2	5	2	14	9	6	30
Broader benefit	2	9	7	32	10	8	36
Financial health	2	9	6	30	10	7	34
Organization development	2	8	5	26	8	5	26
Board oversight	1	7	8	15	8	9	17
Totals	100	138	121	1,752	151	135	1,888
Total possible weighted score				2,000			2,000
Percentage agreement				88%			94%

environment. In the past, the foundation primarily supported innovative programming or general operations. A recent assessment of the local nonprofit community, however, indicates that many of the organizations need to build internal management capacity. As many have grown, they have not put into place the required systems to carry out the business of the organization: managing information, carrying out and using market research to inform their programming, developing consistent internal program planning and budgeting, and having in place standard organization and program evaluation systems. As a result, Mr. Wheeler proposes to the board a two-year grant program, the Innovation Fund, which will in itself be a pilot project intended to help local organizations carefully introduce new management practices. Given the well-documented needs in the community, the board approves the program on a two-year experimental basis: $75,000 to be awarded in the first year and $100,000 to be awarded in the second year if the program is successful.

Mr. Wheeler has long had an interest in venture philanthropy—approaches to giving based on venture capital models. He sees the Innovation Fund as the foundation's approach to early-stage investment. That is, the funding can be used for feasibility studies and piloting new ideas. Mr. Wheeler is familiar with the critical decision matrix and believes that because it was developed from investment due diligence practices, it is a good tool for evaluating Innovation Fund proposals.

Because the given pool of money—$75,000 in the first year and $100,000 in the second—is intended to cover both feasibility and pilot projects, the matrix provides a way of allocating the funds fairly across both categories. And because the weighting system results in a percentage agreement score from 0 to 100 percent in both cases, the projects can be compared easily. For example, if a feasibility proposal scores 75 percent and a pilot proposal scores 55 percent, the feasibility proposal has a better chance of success and is therefore a better investment of the fund's resources.

In both the first and second years, the goal is to allocate the funds to the highest-scoring proposals until the funds are exhausted. There is no limit on the amount requested per proposal or the number of grants awarded. In this way, Mr. Wheeler hopes to promote careful project design along with realistic and accurate budgeting. It has been his experience that many local organizations routinely apply for funds in excess of what they need, on the assumption that they will most likely be awarded less. And in some cases, organizations systematically budget less than is required to carry out the project, assuming that the lower the budget, the more reasonable and frugal they will appear, and this will increase their chances of getting a grant. Prospective grantees are invited to an information session where the purpose of the fund is discussed, the due diligence criteria are reviewed, and the allocation of awards is explained.

The information session proves to be a learning experience for both the grantees and Mr. Wheeler. Most of the applicants are comfortable with the approach and simply ask questions of clarification about the due diligence criteria. The key question the group has is, "Do we have to submit a feasibility proposal and complete that study before we can submit a pilot proposal?" Mr. Wheeler points out that this is not a requirement if the organization has already done its homework and has thoroughly evaluated an idea and judged it to be feasible. When that is the case, the group can move straight to the pilot but should document the feasibility process.

One of the things Mr. Wheeler omits from the presentation is the weighting of the due diligence criteria. This is something he grappled with. He did not want the applicants to force their proposals to meet the criteria and the weights he assigned. Instead, he wants the proposals to accurately reflect each organization's own priorities. Two things specifically excluded are building projects and direct deficit and endowment funding. He provides the applicants with a list and detailed description of the criteria and stresses that he does not expect every proposal to meet every one of the criteria. For example, if the innovation doesn't call for collaboration, they should not add a collaborative component just because it's on the list. But if the proposal is collaborative, the organizations should justify exactly why it is going to be more productive as a group undertaking. Again, the potential applicants are comfortable with this approach, and most believe that they can make use of the fund to support activities that they have already discussed or planned.

Prior to receiving the grant proposals, Mr. Wheeler assigns weights to the due diligence criteria for both the feasibility and pilot matrices. In weighting the feasibility matrix, he stresses strategic alignment, feasibility, organizational fit, measurable impact, and appropriate scope, which are critical to building appropriate and sustainable management systems. His weightings for the feasibility matrix along with his reasons for assigning specific weights can be found in Exhibit 6.3.

Moving to the pilot matrix, Mr. Wheeler changes his weightings to reflect the elements he considers key to successfully acting on a feasible idea. The most heavily weighted are strategic alignment, feasibility, and practicality. These are followed by

Exhibit 6.3. Mr. Wheeler's Feasibility Weightings.

Criteria	Weight	Rationale/Comments
Strategic alignment	12	Should enhance the grantee's ability to fulfill its mission and goals
Feasibility	12	Should be implemented elsewhere or be well reasoned
Expertise	8	Skills sets required should be spelled out in detail
Reasonable cost	8	Budgets should be precise and based on full loaded costs
Fit	12	Effects on ongoing operations should be addressed
Measurable impact	12	Should include detailed evaluation plan
Appropriate scope	12	Should be appropriate in terms of organization size
Personnel	6	Which staff will be involved and why should be listed
Practicality	2	Should not overly strain organization's current operations
Measurable productivity	4	Should result in enhanced capacity and productivity
Risk factors	2	Should be able to articulate potential downside to the project
Collaboration	2	Any collaborations should enhance productivity for all involved
Broader benefit	2	Should include a brief dissemination plan
Financial health	2	Limited discussion of long-term financial impact
Organization development	2	Limited discussion of long-term impact on management capacity
Board oversight	2	Limited discussion of board role in the project
Total	**100**	

expertise, reasonable cost, fit, measurable impact, and appropriate scope. His weightings for the pilot matrix along with the rationale for each are presented in Exhibit 6.4.

Mr. Wheeler receives fifteen proposals: twelve feasibility proposals and three pilot proposals. The proposals, categories, amounts, and brief project descriptions are listed in Table 6.1.

Mr. Wheeler then submits the proposals for review to a three-person panel of nonprofit management experts who will use the matrices to score them independently and then meet to review the scores and make a final recommendation to the foundation. A summary of their scores reflecting percentage agreement is presented in Table 6.2.

Based on the raw results, they would be able to fully fund nine proposals: six feasibility and three pilot projects. However, the last proposal that would make the cut, number 9 in the rankings (the fundraising software feasibility study), has an average percentage agreement score of 71. The project preceding it, number 8 (the shared services feasibility study), has a significantly higher score of 81. When the reviewers meet to discuss the results with Mr. Wheeler, they agree that there are significant issues with the ninth project, specifically in the area of appropriate budget and scope. As a result, the group recommends that they fund only the proposals ranked 1 through 8, for a total of $71,080 in grant awards. They also suggest reallocating the remaining $3,920 of this year's grant funds to the next year's funds, modestly increasing it to $103,920. Mr. Wheeler takes the panel's recommendations to the board. They approve the eight Innovation Fund grants and agree to reallocate the remaining money.

In the second year, three of the feasibility proposals funded in the first year result in viable concepts, and those organizations apply to the Innovation Fund for pilot funds. One of the pilots is successful as well, and that organization will be applying to other foundations to support broader implementation and staff training. These results suggest to Mr. Wheeler that the foundation should expand the Innovation Fund to include later stages of investment. He brings this recommendation to the board, and once again, based on the results from their own two-year pilot of the fund, they agree.

Exhibit 6.4. Mr. Wheeler's Pilot Weightings.

Criteria	Weight	Rationale/Comments
Strategic alignment	12	Actions should clearly support organization's mission and goals
Feasibility	12	Should be based on thorough feasibility assessment
Expertise	8	Necessary expertise should be available and affordable
Reasonable cost	8	The budget is precise, complete, and realistic, with detailed narrative
Fit	8	How the pilot will support the organization's other activities is clear
Measurable impact	8	A detailed evaluation plan is included
Appropriate scope	8	Size is appropriate in terms of anticipated results and resources allocated
Personnel	6	Staff time and expertise are budgeted precisely and appropriately
Practicality	12	There are compelling reasons for why this is a good idea right now
Measurable productivity	4	Reasonable anticipated increase in productivity quantified
Risk factors	4	Risk factors outlined along with planned courses of corrective action
Collaboration	2	If pilot is collaborative, roles and responsibilities clearly delineated
Broader benefit	2	Detailed dissemination plan included
Financial health	2	Discussion of pilot's impact on organization's short- and long-term finances
Organization development	2	Discussion of pilot's impact on long-term impact on management capacity
Board oversight	2	Clear links between board processes and pilot activities and outcome
Total	**100**	

Table 6.1. Summary of Innovation Fund Proposals.

Category	Amount	Description
Feasibility	$30,000	Consultation with a local architecture firm for planning to improve office space allocation
	$3,500	Assessment of fundraising software and related training packages
	$12,420	To work with a communications consultant to look at how best to link satellite offices
	$4,800	To study outsourcing administrative functions
	$10,400	To study the costs and benefits of data mining to better understand audience dynamics
	$8,360	Collaborative group of agencies to explore the feasibility of shared services
	$2,600	Two theaters jointly examining the possible cost saving of shared warehouse space
	$8,800	Study of the cost of developing custom fundraising software for small agency
	$5,430	Analysis of the costs and benefits of moving support staff to satellite program locations
	$6,200	Assess establishing an ongoing market research relationship with a local university
Pilot	$8,500	Install new database software in one department as a test
	$12,040	Outsourcing bookkeeping for one year
	$7,950	Test effectiveness of flexible scheduling for employees
	$14,650	Implement project management system in one program team
	$35,440	Pilot cross-marketing strategy for two organizations serving same population
Total	**$171,090**	

Table 6.2. Summary of Reviewer Scores: Innovation Fund Feasibility and Pilot Proposals.

Rank	Proposal	Type	Amount	Reviewer 1	Reviewer 2	Reviewer 3	Average
1	Data mining	Feasibility	$10,400	98%	95%	89%	94%
2	Database test	Pilot	$8,500	96	90	86	91
3	Shared warehouse	Feasibility	$2,600	92	90	87	90
4	Linking satellite offices	Feasibility	$12,420	93	90	85	89
5	Flexible scheduling	Pilot	$7,950	89	82	80	84
6	Research relationship	Feasibility	$6,200	85	84	80	83
7	Project management	Pilot	$14,650	87	82	80	83
8	Shared services	Feasibility	$8,360	86	80	76	81
9	Fundraising software	Feasibility	$3,500	78	70	65	71
10	Outsourcing study	Feasibility	$4,800	76	60	55	64
11	Moving staff	Feasibility	$5,430	72	63	42	59
12	Custom software	Feasibility	$8,800	60	55	58	58
13	Outsourcing bookkeeping	Pilot	$12,040	55	40	32	42
14	Cross marketing	Pilot	$35,440	40	25	18	28
15	Space planning	Feasibility	$30,000	35	30	12	26

7

Stage Three: Implementation

I dream, I test my dreams against my beliefs, I dare to take risks, and I execute my vision to make those dreams come true.

—*Walt Disney*

ONCE THE PILOT STAGE is complete and the results have been reviewed and evaluated, it's time to consider full implementation. In some cases, the pilot might reveal that the idea is not right for the nonprofit; it might not have the desired impact, or it might put too much of a burden on the organization's operations and resources. In other cases, the results might support moving forward with the idea and provide information that can be used to refine and enhance its implementation.

In the implementation stage, the scope of the change increases. In the previous chapter, we discussed scope in terms of the resources and time required to put the idea into action. What has been tested in a limited part of the organization or community is going to be expanded to other areas. More of the organization's resources will be drawn on, and a greater impact is anticipated. In other words, both the potential risks and the potential benefits increase. Furthermore, with full implementation, there is the underlying assumption that the change will be permanent.

Before deciding to move on to this next stage, the decision makers should test the idea one more time, based on the results of the pilot and any subsequent changes in the organization, environment, or community. With this information, they should reconsider the possible consequences of fully executing their vision. A well-thought-out implementation decision is crucial to a sustainable change that will benefit the organization and community in the long term.

This chapter begins with a discussion of how an organization moves from pilot to implementation. Learning from the pilot is the key to developing a comprehensive implementation plan that provides for sustaining the positive impact while addressing any problems that might emerge. Therefore, we discuss the elements of a good implementation plan with particular attention to how the plan is managed through phasing, careful timing, and systematic assessment. Then we lay out and discuss the matrix tool and due diligence criteria for implementation decisions. We conclude with two minicases that illustrate how the matrix tool can be used to support implementation decisions.

From Pilot to Implementation

> *Zeus does not bring all men's plans to fulfillment.*
> —Homer, **The Iliad**

Success can be dangerous and seductive. If a new idea is piloted successfully, decision makers are often tempted to move directly to full implementation. They have the evidence that shows the new idea has worked—albeit in a limited and highly controlled application—and so can once again become excited and optimistic. In other words, they can easily slip into reactive decision making. However, in going from test project to full-scale and permanent implementation, they should ask a number of questions. As with pilot decisions, if they do not examine the next step carefully before going forward, they can put the organization at risk. A structured due diligence process at the implementation stage can reveal more about the potential benefits and pitfalls that might result.

What's more, they should keep in mind that even if the pilot has been highly successful, it might be perfectly reasonable to forgo implementation entirely, postpone it, or limit its scope, depending on what comes out of the due diligence process. Once a new idea has been demonstrated to be feasible, the next step is to determine whether it is appropriate for the organization to implement the idea and to what extent. The results of a successful pilot looked at in isolation might support implementation, but other factors might make implementation impractical. An internal problem, such as turnover in key personnel, might delay implementation. Or an external change, such as a shift in funder policy, might reduce the organization's resources to the point that the change becomes impossible. In addition to what the decision makers learn from the pilot, they should reassess any changes in the organization's internal capacity and its external support before moving forward. Their decision must be guided by one central question: Is it practical for this organization to fully implement this idea at this time?

In determining if and how the idea should be implemented, the decision makers should once again revisit the concepts of risk, leverage, and sustainability. More of the organization is involved in the change during implementation, and especially in the case of new programming, more of the community is also directly affected.

As we have already explained, the greater the scope of the change is, the greater the resources involved and the greater the potential risks are. Scope affects leverage. Managers often assume that the greater the scope of the change, the greater the leverage achieved through economies of scale will be. This is not necessarily the case. The costs of managing and coordinating expanded activities are often underestimated, which can affect both efficiency and effectiveness.

Finally, the issue of sustainability now takes on greater importance. A good pilot focuses on risk and leverage, but only for the limited time of the project. Because full implementation makes the change permanent, sustainability and resources become major issues.

In some cases, pilot projects demonstrate that an idea will have even greater benefit or broader application than originally anticipated. Other pilots indicate that the original idea can be improved and made more relevant and successful. The information gleaned from the pilot, as well as from any additional internal and external assessments, should be used to develop the full-scale implementation plan. Similar to the plan used to support the pilot decision, the implementation plan should outline anticipated internal and external impact, the required resources, and how the change will be managed and assessed over time. In other words, the plan should clearly outline the measurable goals, include a comprehensive budget, and provide clear guidelines for the ongoing management of the change.

A Good Implementation Plan

Plans are only good intentions unless they immediately degenerate into hard work.

—*Peter Drucker*

Whereas the pilot is a project with a distinct beginning, middle, and end, implementation results in a permanent change that is managed continuously. The implementation plan is not a project plan; it is a long-term action plan that incorporates processes for ongoing monitoring and management. Managing the implementation of a critical decision over time is hard and complex work.

As with the pilot, multiple stakeholders should be involved in the development of the implementation plan: people who were involved in the design, implementation, and evaluation of the pilot; people who will be involved in the implementation and ongoing assessment processes; and people with specialized knowledge or experience directly related to putting the idea into widespread practice. We'll take the example of implementing a new computer system throughout the organization. Rolling out a new system to an entire organization will involve those who tested it in its limited use in the pilot, those who originally proposed the idea in the information technology department, groups of end users who will now be affected, and external hardware and software consultants.

Just as we have staged the due diligence process to deal with complex decisions, staging—or phasing—implementation is one way to minimize risk and learn about how the idea plays out in practice in a controlled way.

The computer system can be phased in department by department over the course of several months. During early phases, staff can identify issues—for example, weaknesses in the training program—that inform the subsequent phases. Phasing also allows the timing of the implementation to be more malleable. By organizing the work in discrete segments, the organization can manage it without stopping progress.

A detailed implementation plan includes a time line with distinct phases organizing specific activities and intermediate goals. This allows the decision makers, along with those working directly on implementing the change, to monitor the results. The plan should establish points for assessing actual outcomes. Periodic review processes provide opportunities to make corrections or improvements as implementation progresses.

The budget for the full implementation should include the costs of putting the idea into place as well as the costs of sustaining it over time. A detailed analysis of the costs and available resources will provide a good basis for understanding what it takes to move forward. And comparing the amount budgeted with the intended impact will give a precise estimate of what the leverage will be. Finally, weighing the funds required for implementation against the operating budget will give an indicator of fit and sustainability. This last check is important because sometimes a project that is manageable as a pilot can overwhelm an organization in full implementation.

Whether implementation supports the nonprofit's overall strategy is the ultimate test of its value to the organization and community. The implementation plan should therefore contain a detailed process for monitoring, assessment, and evaluation, along with specific criteria for measuring success and failure. This will include the expected outcomes at various stages of implementation and the ongoing impact and productivity gains anticipated. The appropriate individuals should be assigned the responsibility of collecting and analyzing the required assessment data as implementation progresses.

With this general set of guidelines for implementation, we can move on to explore how to use the matrix to help organize the due diligence process.

The Implementation Matrix

The most decisive actions of our life—I mean those that are most likely to decide the whole course of our future—are, more often than not, unconsidered.

—André Gide

The implementation matrix presented in Exhibit 7.1 has one fewer criterion than the feasibility or pilot matrices. "Feasibility" is omitted because if the pilot has been successful and the organization is ready to move to the implementation stage, it is clear that what is proposed can be done. It's feasible. The implementation matrix uses the remaining criteria to determine whether the idea is practical for the organization on a larger scale and for the long term. Decision makers should use the due diligence criteria to review the proposed change's compatibility with the organization's current and future strategy, operations, and resources. The guiding questions for the implementation stage address overall organizational and community impact and requirements for sustaining the change over time. Once again, the weighting of each question is dependent on the specific organization's situation, goals, and priorities and should be carried out by the key decision maker in consultation with the appropriate individuals and groups.

A set of questions follows each of the fifteen criteria to guide decision makers in scoring. They are intended to help develop a balanced understanding of why full implementation might or might not be wise. In the process of reviewing and discussing the criteria, the decision makers can also use results to reassess and, if needed, modify the implementation plan before action is taken.

Strategic Alignment

Implementation should help advance the organization in ways that are consistent with its strategic plan. Because putting the idea in place permanently will result in both short- and long-term changes, the implementation plan should be closely reviewed and compared with the organization's strategic and operational planning documents. There should be a clear fit with the specific values, vision, mission, goals, objectives, and priorities.

Exhibit 7.1. Sample Implementation Matrix.			
Criteria	Weight	Decision Maker Score	Weighted Score
Strategic alignment	15		
Fit	12		
Practicality	12		
Measurable impact	12		
Reasonable cost	10		
Appropriate scope	10		
Measurable productivity	8		
Expertise	4		
Risk factors	4		
Personnel	4		
Collaboration	2		
Broader benefit	2		
Financial health	2		
Organization development	2		
Board oversight	1		
Totals	100		
Total possible weighted score			1,000
Percentage agreement			%

In some situations, an innovation might significantly contribute to the strategy of the nonprofit in its limited pilot form but limit the organization if carried out fully. For example, wholesale implementation of a new computer system with customized organization-specific database software might support the strategic objectives of the development department by enhancing operations and accountability to donors. Departments directly related to the delivery of service, however, might already have adequate software packages and would benefit only marginally from the hardware upgrade. In this case, moving to a new and unproven system might cause unnecessary disruptions in service. Developing a comprehensive computer system and implementing it across the organization would amount to reinventing the wheel for these departments, and it might actually impede the organization from pursuing its mission. In this example, the implementation plans would probably have to be rethought and scaled back to maintain strategic fit.

Questions to Ask to Assess Strategic Alignment

☑ How, specifically, will the full implementation enhance the organization's current role in the community, reflected in its vision, mission, goals, and values?

☑ How will full implementation fit within the organization's existing strategic and operating plans? Which specific goals and activities does it support? How does it support them? Is it better for some areas than others? What will have to be amended in the implementation plan to result in the best fit?

☑ What is the potential strategic impact of full implementation? That is, does implementation significantly enhance the organization's ability to pursue major high-priority action items that will have a major effect on the organization overall? How will it do so? Or will it only marginally contribute to minor, low-priority items that affect only specific programs or departments?

The greater the anticipated strategic impact is, the higher the decision makers' scores will be.

Fit

Full implementation will have both long- and short-term effects on the organization's operations and its relationships with outside stakeholders. The greater the anticipated impact is, the better the fit must be, both internally and externally. The implementation plan should address the full range of intended benefits for the nonprofit and the community. It should also anticipate negative consequences and lay out means of dealing with them.

In terms of internal operations, the implementation plan and time line should detail how the new activities will be introduced. A plan that works out staff assignments, space and equipment utilization, and scheduling will smooth the impact on existing programs and processes.

The anticipated impact on the broader community should also be addressed. With the findings of the initial feasibility assessment in mind, and the results of the pilot, and any subsequent changes or developments in the community, take into account the needs and concerns of the relevant stakeholders. The stakeholder groups include consumers of the organization's programs and services, other nonprofit organizations that may be affected, and funders.

Questions to Ask to Assess Fit

☑ How does full implementation fit within the organization's annual operating plans? Successful implementation should support specific programmatic or administrative goals. Identify who will carry out the implementation and how it will affect existing workloads and job assignments in the short and long terms. Determine the impact of reallocating resources, such as space and equipment, to the new activity as opposed to their normal use. Finally, to prevent conflicts, review the proposed timing of the implementation in terms of the organization's routine activity levels.

☑ How will implementation affect the community? Answering this question requires an understanding of the external stakeholders, their goals and needs, their reactions to the pilot, and their assumptions about broader implementation. Decision makers might consult with specific groups of clients or audience members, other nonprofits, and funders.

The better the fit is with internal operations and the activities and interests of external stakeholders, the higher the decision makers' scores will be.

Practicality

The decision makers should revisit how practical the implementation plan is in terms of the nonprofit's current situation. Perhaps conditions have changed since the pilot, so it is not good for the organization to move ahead with the idea. There can be other signs too that the organization should limit implementation. For example, whereas the pilot might have demonstrated that an outreach program was feasible when tested at one site, the implementation plan proposes that the program be expanded to six sites in the community. But reduced funding and the scarcity of good locations might make it practical at this time to limit the program to only four sites.

Question to Ask to Assess Practicality

☑ Should the nonprofit implement the idea at this time? If so, should it be implemented fully or partially? What, internally or externally, prevents the nonprofit from implementing at this time? Should the idea be considered at a later date?

If decision makers determine that the idea has been demonstrated to be practical in the pilot and internal and external conditions continue to support the concept, the higher their scores will be.

Measurable Impact

Implementation should result in significant changes in programming or operations. A set of specific measurements tied to organizational goals is required to assess whether the changes are effective and to what extent. The measurements will most likely be similar, if not identical, to those developed for the pilot. The measures provide clear indicators of how actual organizational performance is affected and how much it differs from the outcomes anticipated in the implementation plan. Objectively determining positive impact and negative consequences provides a way of monitoring, assessing, and managing the effectiveness of the implementation over time.

Questions to Ask to Assess Impact

☑ What are the specific positive changes that should result from implementation? The intended changes should be clearly articulated in terms of what implementation might increase, decrease, or maintain.

☑ How will impact be measured? Establish quantitative indicators, and provide a way to monitor them. Set a target number within a specific time frame to serve as a baseline for success as implementation proceeds.

The clearer and more precise the measures are, the higher the decision makers' scores will be.

Reasonable Cost

As the scale of the change increases, so do the costs. While the cost of the pilot might have been reasonable, budgeting for full implementation might reveal that the nonprofit cannot afford the change. There is also the danger of underbudgeting. For a limited project, underbudgeting bears only the risk of limited failure and impact. But for expanded, long-term activities, underbudgeting can create too great a risk to reasonably accept.

A comprehensive analysis of costs and budget projections should be part of the implementation plan. This is particularly important if the implementation is going to be phased. If the implementation is to proceed in stages, the costs of each stage should be developed along with the costs of coordinating the process. In some cases, segmenting the process can significantly increase costs. For example, major building projects are often phased and accordingly bear increased costs because of the additional setup work associated with starting and stopping, the higher price of supplies purchased in multiple smaller quantities, and the effect of inflation on financing.

Questions to Ask to Assess Cost

☑ What are all the costs of fully implementing and sustaining this proposed idea? Work out a budget that includes direct and indirect costs, fixed and variable costs, and sunk versus relevant costs. In a detailed narrative, support each line item.

☑ Are the budgeted amounts realistic? The decision makers should review the assumptions made about the costs in each budget line to determine if they are based on actual costs in the local marketplace.

☑ Where will the budgeted resources come from? Each line item should be tied to a reliable source of funds. If the items are tied to current income streams and existing resources, will there be enough money for the new program as well as the activities traditionally funded through these sources? If implementation depends on new dollars, have they been secured? If not, what are the potential sources of funding and the timing for developing an adequate support base? What are the contingencies if the new sources do not pan out?

The more the decision makers know about the real costs and the more accurate and reasonable the implementation budget is, the higher their scores will be.

Appropriate Scope

The magnitude of the innovation must be taken into account to determine whether the organization has the experience, infrastructure, or resource base to undertake and sustain it. While a limited pilot project might have been relatively easy to manage and support, expanding the activity might burden or overwhelm the organization. Review of the earlier criteria—in particular, discussions of fair and reasonable cost—provides a basis for understanding whether the scope of full implementation is appropriate.

Question to Ask to Assess Scope

☑ Are the resources budgeted for implementation disproportionate to the operating budget of the organization?

The smaller the implementation budget is relative to the operating budget, the higher the decision makers' scores will be.

Measurable Productivity

Full implementation should result in increased efficiency. In other words, once the new idea has been put into practice, the nonprofit should be able to do more with its resources. For example, when a new computer system is installed and the staff is trained and comfortable working with the new equipment, information should be processed and communicated more quickly and accurately than in the past. Dividing results obtained by the resources expended provides the key ratio.

In addition, the decision makers should have an idea of how much return can be expected from the effort and resources invested throughout the implementation process. Early phases might require a greater concentration of effort and resources.

Questions to Ask to Assess Productivity

☑ Will successful implementation have a measurable impact on the productivity of the organization? If so, the positive or negative impact should be defined in a measurable way. Also, in cases where considerable resources are expended in an early phase but are no longer required in later phases, any differences in productivity gains over the course of the implementation should be assessed.

☑ Will increased productivity in one area be offset by a decrease in productivity in another area? For example, a new computer system might require the information technology department to add more staff to assist in training and support.

The greater the anticipated increase in measurable productivity is, the higher the decision makers' scores will be.

Expertise

A considerable portion of the cost and effort in introducing a new idea can be tied to bringing in new skills, a major portion of the start-up cost. If knowledge is successfully transferred to the nonprofit early on, there is a greater chance of success at a lower cost. In some cases, however, ongoing support is required to sustain the change over time.

Questions to Ask to Assess Expertise

☑ What specialized expertise is necessary to implement and support the idea? Describe the needed programmatic, administrative, and technical skills, and plan the role they will play in the implementation process over time.

☑ Where will the expertise come from? Does the expertise already exist within the staff? If so, identify the people who have it, and detail their roles in the process.

☑ If the expertise must be obtained from outside the organization, is it readily available in the current labor market or pools of volunteers? If it must come from an external source through hiring additional staff or consultants or through volunteer involvement, how will these people be recruited? The implementation plan should provide specific job descriptions and qualifications, including a recruitment strategy for bringing in the appropriate specialists.

☑ If the expertise must be obtained from external sources, will there be sufficient transfer of knowledge for the organization to sustain the innovation without again going to the outside? Ideally the knowledge necessary for successful implementation should become resident within the organization. The implementation plan should provide a method for transferring the knowledge to the current staff if that is possible. Otherwise it should provide for additional staff or contractual or volunteer arrangements on an ongoing basis.

☑ What will be the cost?

The greater the availability, affordability, and transferability of expertise are, the higher the decision makers' scores will be.

Risk Factors

The decision makers should review what could go wrong and assess how well equipped the organization is to correct potential problems. As in the pilot project, the same types of risk should be addressed: technological, personnel, financial, and market.

Question to Ask to Assess Risk

☑ What might prevent successful implementation? Pay attention specifically to technological, personnel, financial, and market risks. The decision makers should once again develop a range of what-if scenarios in each area and determine how the organization might respond to any damage. If adequate safeguards are in place, the risks can be managed.

The fewer the potential risks and the better the organization is able to manage them if they do occur, the higher the decision makers' scores will be.

Personnel

The issue of personnel has already come into the discussion of expertise, cost, and fit in both the feasibility and the pilot matrices. Specific skill sets will also be needed to implement and manage the actual change. Detailed plans should be drawn up for staffing changes, including reassignments and the addition of newly hired employees.

Questions to Ask to Assess Personnel

☑ Does the organization have the appropriate personnel to implement and sustain the new idea once it is implemented? If so, the staff with the requisite skills should then be assigned to their roles within the implementation process. If people must be recruited from the outside, develop job descriptions, determine their availability, and calculate the costs of recruiting and hiring them.

☑ Does the organization have the appropriate personnel to manage the implementation and sustain the changes? Sometimes the effort required to administer and monitor the change is not taken into account. Managing implementation has both internal and external dimensions, such as integrating new activities with other parts of the organization's operations and managing stakeholder relations.

The greater the availability of qualified personnel is, the higher the decision makers' scores will be.

Collaboration

The collaboration of multiple organizations in the implementation can provide an opportunity to build and sustain community, combine limited resources, and promote ongoing learning.

Questions to Ask to Assess Collaboration

☑ Can the proposed concept be effectively used and sustained by more than one organization? If so, identify these organizations, and assess the benefits to them. Consider discussions with pilot and other potential partners, as well as reviews of their current and planned operations and programming.

☑ How can organizations best pool resources to achieve the greatest benefit? This will require advance planning for how the organizations will work together to fully implement and sustain the collaboration. For each partner, outline roles, responsibilities, resources, and anticipated outcomes.

The greater the number of viable collaborators and the better developed the goals and plans for working together are, the higher the decision makers' scores will be.

Broader Benefit

This criterion addresses the range of organizations that might ultimately benefit once the new idea has been implemented. The idea might be viable and productive in other organizational settings.

Questions to Ask to Assess the Broader Benefit

☑ If the idea is successfully implemented, do benefits extend beyond the organization? As with collaboration, spell out the benefits in detail, and identify the other organizations that might adopt the idea.

☑ How will the benefits be publicized and shared? Detailed dissemination plans should be developed.

The greater the number of organizations identified and the more specific the dissemination plans are, the higher the decision makers' scores will be.

Financial Health

The new idea, once fully implemented, should strengthen the financial health of the organization. It should support the organization's long-term ability to generate income, earned and unearned. As we discussed earlier, there might be a short-term financial burden in the early phases of the implementation process, but this should be offset by the anticipated benefits over time.

Question to Ask to Assess Financial Health

☑ How will successful implementation contribute to both the short- and long-term financial health of the organization? Just as in the pilot stage, this question is best answered by modeling the costs and revenues associated with implementation over time. The more precise the understanding of the impact on the finances is, the better the assessment.

The greater the long- and short-term financial benefits, the higher the decision makers' scores will be.

Organization Development

In addition to contributing to the organization's overall financial health, implementation should support its future growth and development in other ways too. An innovative process or program can position an organization for more and better work in the future.

Question to Ask to Assess Organization Development

☑ How will the successful implementation of the new idea contribute to the development of the organization in the following areas: staff, both personally and professionally; program; and administration? Ideally, the decision should expand staff members' skills as well as meet their personal and professional goals. A new idea that is at odds with their goals will create a significant problem. If the innovation is tied to programming, it should enhance the organization's existing and planned activities by increasing content, quality, or reach. If the change is administrative, it should have the potential for making the organization's work processes more efficient and effective.

The more the implementation of the idea contributes to staff, program, and administrative development, the higher the decision makers' scores will be.

Board Oversight

Full implementation should fit with ongoing board review processes and committee structures. Appropriate plans and policies should be in place to guide how the implementation is carried out and how it is monitored over time.

Questions to Ask to Assess Board Oversight

☑ Does the board have in place the appropriate committees, processes, and policies to oversee implementation?

☑ Are board members directly involved in implementation, and does this complement or conflict with their oversight roles? In cases of potential conflict, develop appropriate checks and balances.

The more closely matched the implementation process is with existing board oversight mechanisms and the more clearly defined the board members' involvement is, the higher the decision makers' scores will be.

———————————

The following minicases provide examples of how the matrix can be used to support full implementation of an idea that has been successfully piloted. The first focuses on senior staff in the review of a major operational change, and the second examines board and staff as they assess a major strategic shift.

THE CASE OF THE COMMUNITY SENIOR CENTER

I do not fear computers; I fear the lack of them.

—*Isaac Asimov*

The Community Senior Center is a thriving and growing nonprofit in a small town. It provides a broad range of programming: a wellness center, human services and support groups, cultural events, education and training, and nutrition counseling. The center has grown steadily over the past ten years as the local population has aged. By developing well-targeted programming with the help of its advisory council, the organization has been successful in meeting the increasing demand. The quality of the programming has resulted in a good relationship with a diverse group of funders. With this strong position in the community, the executive director and development staff have been able to raise the money they need to expand the facilities and recruit personnel and volunteers.

The center is working to coordinate its activities better. As part of this administrative work, the staff has been moving from a combination of computer and paper systems for program scheduling to a fully integrated automated system. Much of the past year was spent working with a computer consultant and testing a portion of the system in the wellness center. At this point a plan has been developed for installing the system in the remaining program areas.

Mr. Charles, the center's executive director, realizes that the system will have to function across a number of program and administrative areas that have different work processes and departmental cultures. He is the person who will ultimately make the decision for and bear the responsibility of implementing the system. To get an idea of how well the system will work across the organization, he decides to follow the due diligence process using the implementation matrix.

First, Mr. Charles assigns weights to the scores based on his broad understanding of the center's history, future strategy, and current operations. Then he convenes a working group consisting of himself, Ms. Brown, the director of programs, and Mr. Scott, the computer systems manager, to review the implementation plan using the decision matrix. In this way, he will involve the individuals with the most program and technical knowledge in the decision process. Their perspectives complement his own, and they will be key to installing and managing the system if he makes the decision to go ahead. Each member of the working group assigns scores to the matrix individually. Then they meet to share and discuss the results so that Mr. Charles can make the final decision. This is how their scores compare:

Strategic alignment. Implementation of the automated system is consistent with the strategic goal of instituting best administrative practices throughout the center. It is one of the major goals that has been driving a range of management changes across departments since the development of the plan. Charles's score: 10, Brown's score: 10, Scott's score: 10.

Fit. The pilot was very successful with the wellness staff. The computer manager will be able to make all the required changes and schedule the installation in a way that minimally disrupts the operation. Nevertheless, some older staff and volunteers who currently track program data for the cultural events and education programs have voiced opposition to the change. These individuals have no computer experience and are comfortable with the existing paper system. In terms of external stakeholders, the program information is especially useful to funders and local policymakers, and automating collection will enable the center to meet their demands for timelier reporting. Charles's score: 8, Brown's score: 7, Scott's score: 9.

Practicality. The pilot was very successful. Now that program data can be collected consistently and in a timely manner, reports to external funders and supporters can be developed more quickly. In addition, the new system has made it possible for the wellness center coordinator to use the data for more efficient scheduling and staff assignments. The same benefits will most likely be realized in other program areas when the new system is in place. The funds for full implementation have been secured, and the prices of the hardware and software have actually dropped since the system was designed. Charles's score: 10, Brown's score: 10, Scott's score: 10.

Measurable impact. The new system in the wellness center has resulted in the adoption of a best practice, and as a consequence, facilities, program time, and staff are used more efficiently than in the past. The new system also enables the staff to track which programs are growing in popularity and which have declining enrollments. By correlating this with evaluation information, the staff is beginning to develop a continuous improvement system. Charles's score: 10, Brown's score: 10, Scott's score: 10.

Reasonable cost. The system is projected to cost less than originally budgeted because the costs of the hardware and software have gone down—not uncommon in the development of management information systems. Charles's score: 10, Brown's score: 10, Scott's score: 10.

Appropriate scope. All of the programs at the center are structured and administered in the same way and serve the same basic client group. By implementing the system fully, the center will be able to monitor, compare, and report program performance for the entire organization. Charles's score: 10, Brown's score: 10, Scott's score: 10.

Measurable productivity. Based on tracking studies done by Ms. Brown and the wellness center coordinator, the staff at the wellness center can enter and manage data twice as quickly using the new system. In the pilot, the new system replaced a less powerful and less user-friendly database program. Because the new system will replace similar systems in other program areas, along with the even less efficient paper systems, it is assumed that the increase in productivity will be at least twofold throughout the center. Charles's score: 10, Brown's score: 10, Scott's score: 10.

Expertise. Mr. Scott understands the technical requirements of the new system, and the wellness center staff understands how the application supports the center's programming. Together they are capable of implementing it across the organization without relying on external support. Charles's score: 10, Brown's score: 10, Scott's score: 10.

Risk factors. Mr. Scott is the only staff member with the necessary computer expertise to manage the system. This creates a potential risk if he were to leave the center. But in that case, an external consultant could be hired, so it is a risk that can be managed. There is no other apparent risk. Charles's score: 9, Brown's score: 9, Scott's score: 10.

Personnel. Several older people in key program positions do not have experience working with automated systems and are resisting the change. Their resistance will pose a serious problem if it is not resolved prior to implementation. Ms. Brown and Mr. Charles are faced with potentially replacing or reassigning staff and volunteers. Although individuals with the appropriate skills are readily available locally, eliminating older workers is at odds with the center's core values. Charles's score: 5, Brown's score: 3, Scott's score: 7.

Collaboration. There was no collaboration in the pilot or any planned in the full implementation of the system. Charles's score: 0, Brown's score: 0, Scott's score: 0.

Broader benefit. A number of funders have expressed interest in how the system could be used for external reporting. They were impressed with the clarity and detail of the information produced during the pilot. The implementation plan specifies a scheduled information session for funders of local nonprofits so that they become acquainted with the system and the information it can provide. The goal is to teach the local community about the benefits of automating program management. Charles's score: 10, Brown's score: 8, Scott's score: 9.

Financial health. The pilot saved considerable staff time and expense and made a favorable impression on the center's funders. Full implementation should create additional economies and strengthen the center's position with funders. Charles's score: 8, Brown's score: 6, Scott's score: 8.

Organization development. Implementation of the system would result in increasing the staff's technical skills, enabling the organization to better manage its resources and better serve their constituents. The organization's position in the local funding community will improve with better, more detailed reporting. Charles's score: 8, Brown's score: 8, Scott's score: 7.

Board oversight. The pilot was the first large technology project at the center. During the design of the system, Mr. Charles realized that the center needed a technology policy to realize its goal of implementing best practices. One of the board members, who is an executive for a software company, agreed. And an ad hoc committee researched and developed the center's technology policy. The implementation of the new system will be carried out according to the policy. Charles's score: 10, Brown's score: 10, Scott's score: 10.

The summary of the weightings and scores are presented in Exhibit 7.2. Clearly, with 92 percent agreement, the case for implementation is extremely strong. However, attention will have to be given to the fit and personnel issues. It is decided that these issues will be resolved first, and then full implementation will proceed.

Exhibit 7.2. Summary of Mr. Charles's, Ms. Brown's, and Mr. Scott's Scores.

Criteria	Weight	Mr. Charles's Score	Ms. Brown's Score	Mr. Scott's Score	Total Score	Total Weighted Score
Strategic alignment	15	10	10	10	30	450
Fit	12	8	7	9	24	288
Practicality	12	10	10	10	30	360
Measurable impact	12	10	10	10	30	360
Reasonable cost	10	10	10	10	30	300
Appropriate scope	10	10	10	10	30	300
Measurable productivity	8	10	10	10	30	240
Expertise	4	10	10	10	30	120
Risk factors	4	9	9	10	28	112
Personnel	4	5	3	7	15	60
Collaboration	2	0	0	0	0	0
Broader benefit	2	10	8	9	27	54
Financial health	2	8	6	8	22	44
Organization development	2	8	8	7	23	46
Board oversight	1	10	10	10	30	30
Totals	**100**	**128**	**121**	**130**	**379**	**2,764**
Total possible weighted score						**3,000**
Percentage agreement						**92%**

THE CASE OF THE CONNECTED
THEATER COMPANY

All the world's a stage.

—*William Shakespeare*

Connected Theater is an established regional company in a major urban center. Founded twenty years ago by its current artistic director, Mr. Lloyd, and the company's resident playwright, Mr. Samuel, Connected Theater has achieved not only regional but national critical acclaim for its productions, most of which focus on contemporary social and political issues.

The theater has pursued its core mission of developing and presenting productions that address current problems and topics to a regional audience. The company has done this through traditional programming, including a subscription series, readings of new works, and educational programming. As Connected Theater's reputation has grown, regional theaters in the United States have begun to produce its work. Last year the company was invited to present one of its plays at a major festival in Europe, something that Mr. Lloyd and Mr. Samuel had always wanted to do.

The company was able to make the trip with funding from individual supporters of the theater. It was a huge success: every night was sold out, and the company received critical acclaim in the international theater press. The artists met and exchanged ideas with their peers from around the world, and the company returned from the festival energized and excited. This experience marked a turning point for Connected Theater.

Based on the success of this limited experience at the festival, Mr. Lloyd began to think about touring as a way to develop the company further. But he was not thinking of simply adding limited national and international touring to the existing programming mix. He was thinking of repositioning the Connected Theater as a global citizen. International touring would be on a par with its subscription season.

Mr. Lloyd discussed his vision with his board chair, Ms. Evans, a local bank executive. She had been a longtime advocate of the theater and played a major role in its fundraising efforts. Although she was intrigued with the idea and clearly understood how it would advance the organization artistically and increase its market, she felt that this was a decision that the board and company staff would have to assess very carefully, since it would have a major impact on the organization's strategy and operations. Mr. Lloyd agreed and asked for her help in working through the idea.

Ms. Evans, in the course of her career, had had extensive experience in making commercial loans to support business expansion. Connected Theater was facing a similar expansion decision. She viewed the festival experience in Europe as a test of the idea's viability—a pilot. However, she knew that moving from the festival experience to wholesale implementation of a global touring strategy was complex and risky. She decided to subject the idea to a thorough due diligence review, involving key board members as well as senior staff. The group would use the implementation matrix as a way to manage the process and record and present its opinions. Ms. Evans discussed this approach with Mr. Lloyd, and they agreed that this was a good way to proceed. Together the two of them weighted the matrix to ensure that it reflected the organization's strategic, artistic, and operational priorities. Their weightings are summarized in Exhibit 7.3.

Ms. Evans put together a review group that balanced the board perspective with the artistic and operational staff perspective. From the board, she included herself as committee chair; Mr. Robinson, a certified public accountant and board treasurer; and Ms. Marshall, a noted arts educator and chair of the development committee. From the staff, she included Mr. Lloyd, Mr. Samuel, and Mr. Sanders, the business manager. The first charge to the committee was to put together a detailed plan with budgets and time lines for touring. When the plan was completed, each committee member received a copy of it, along with the matrix, and they began their review of the program for global touring. Table 7.1 presents the summary matrix giving the results from all six committee members. The average percentage of agreement is 36 percent.

Using the matrix results, the committee quickly came to consensus on each of the due diligence criteria. The highlights for each criterion follow:

Strategic alignment. The touring plan does not fit with the company's current mission as a regional theater serving primarily a local audience. However, Connected Theater's artistic vision is tied to political and social issues that are increasingly affected by globalization. It might be time to revisit the organization's strategy.

Expertise. Because of the company's limited experience in international programming, it will most likely have to rely on consultants to help with everything from marketing to legal issues related to touring.

Reasonable cost. The costs related to international programming are a major concern. First, the theater does not have established relationships with institutional funders who will support international travel. Second, participation in the European festival was a

Exhibit 7.3. Mr. Lloyd's and Ms. Evans's Implementation Weightings.

Criteria	Weight	Rationale/Comments
Strategic alignment	10	Should be in line with artistic vision and community
Expertise	6	Specialized expertise critical to international programming
Reasonable cost	10	Budget narrative should address sources and international issues
Fit	6	How well the proposed program complements what is in place
Measurable impact	8	Key measures of success included
Appropriate scope	10	Should address theater's ability to manage large-scale change
Personnel	6	How well current staff are prepared to work on international programs
Practicality	10	When and how this might be introduced
Measurable productivity	2	Impact on productivity should be quantified
Risk factors	10	Should address the potential downside of large-scale change
Collaboration	2	Should address any partners
Broader benefit	2	Should address how we will "spread the news"
Financial health	6	Should address impact of major change on theater finances
Organization development	2	How well this positions the theater for the future
Board oversight	10	Should address how well prepared the board is to "go global"
Total	**100**	

Table 7.1. Summary of Committee Members' Scores.

Criteria	Weight	Evans	Robinson	Marshall	Lloyd	Samuel	Sanders
Strategic alignment	10	5	3	6	7	7	5
Expertise	6	2	2	3	4	3	2
Reasonable cost	10	3	1	4	4	4	2
Fit	6	3	1	4	5	5	3
Measurable impact	8	7	4	8	9	8	7
Appropriate scope	10	2	1	4	6	4	3
Personnel	6	2	2	3	4	4	2
Practicality	10	2	0	3	3	3	2
Measurable productivity	2	0	0	2	3	4	2
Risk factors	10	0	0	2	2	3	2
Collaboration	2	0	0	5	4	8	5
Broader benefit	2	2	0	6	5	8	3
Financial health	6	1	0	4	4	5	2
Organization development	2	9	5	10	10	10	7
Board oversight	10	3	2	4	5	5	4

Average % Agreement = 36%

one-time effort supported by individuals who are not capable of sustaining more extensive programming. Third, fluctuations in exchange rates must be taken into account. Currently, the U.S. dollar is in a weak position, increasing potential costs of international programming significantly.

Fit. The company does not have the systems in place to handle the planning and logistics of touring on a regular basis. The change would not directly serve its current local audience base. And none of the existing institutional funders, foundations, and corporations will support international programming. In order to implement the change, the company would have to reorganize its operations, build a new set of relationships with multiple audiences, and develop new sources of funding for international programs. In other words, the fit with the existing theater organization is poor.

Measurable impact. There are clear measures of impact. These include increased audience and additional opportunities for the company's artists.

Appropriate scope. The international programming will be on a par with the theater's subscription series. It will be one of the company's major programs. And when all the costs are taken into account, it will indeed be the largest in terms of resources invested. If Connected Theater were to implement it wholesale, it would overwhelm the organization. Because it is such a broad change, it should be implemented in a series of smaller phases.

Personnel. Current personnel will not be able to manage the new program. Some of the deficiency can be addressed through training; however, additional personnel will be needed to manage the tours, work with presenters and negotiate contracts, and raise funds.

Practicality. Compelling reasons argue in favor of repositioning Connected Theater as a global organization. However, given the issue of fit, it is not practical to do so at this time. The discussion of repositioning should be central in developing the company's next strategic plan, scheduled for the upcoming fiscal year. Given the scope of the change, it should be phased in over a period of several years.

Measurable productivity. It is not clear at this point how implementation will affect productivity in the long run. In the short run, productivity will decline because resources will be committed to developing the touring programming along with the infrastructure needed to support it. There will be no immediate return on this investment.

Risk factors. There is considerable financial and market risk to implementing a touring program. Because it is such a big project, the financial commitment to develop and sustain it is significant. The company will also be marketing its performances to new and diverse audiences. Given the scope of the program, if the programming fails, the company's viability will be threatened.

Collaboration. There are no immediate opportunities for pursuing this as a collaborative program. However, the relationships built during the tours have the potential for creating international collaborations in the future, such as artist exchanges.

Broader benefit. What is learned from the effort can be of use to other regional theaters as they expand. However, the theater has no formal dissemination plans in place.

Financial health. Without financial support, touring undermines the short- and long-term financial health of the organization.

Organization development. The introduction of touring will provide a way for the organization to grow and develop significantly. In particular, it will allow the leadership to expand its current artistic vision, provide opportunities for artists, and expand the theater's audience base.

Board oversight. The board is currently unable to oversee the program adequately. To do so would require changes in committee structure and increased capacity to address liability and risk management issues associated with international organizations.

The matrix summary shows an average percentage agreement of only 36 percent. The low agreement does not, however, result in a decision to abandon the idea and not implement it. There is general agreement that international expansion is the next logical step in Connected Theater's growth and development. But the scope of the change moves it beyond a decision to simply add a new program. It becomes a major strategic decision that means rethinking and redesigning the overall organization, how it is governed, and how it operates. The decision is made that internationally repositioning the theater will become the focus of the next strategic plan. The actual planning process is scheduled to begin in the next year. In advance of that process, the board and staff are charged with collecting the detailed background information about international venues, presenters, costs, legal issues, funding streams, consultants, and other key components that will enable the company to advance in this direction.

8

Stage Four: Cutback

We must be willing to get rid of the life we've planned,
so as to have the life that is waiting for us.

—Joseph Campbell

SOME OF THE MOST DIFFICULT CHOICES to make involve
stopping. This can be especially hard for those who have been doing
something for a long time. In organizations, some practices outlive their
usefulness. Innovative ideas have a life cycle: they progress from feasibility, to
pilot, to full implementation. When an idea that has been fully implemented
is no longer working and managers are faced with putting an end to an existing program or practice, the idea is in the fourth stage in its life cycle: the
end stage. The critical choices made at this stage are cutback decisions.

In cutback situations, the decision makers determine if something the
nonprofit is doing is obsolete. In some cases, this might result in completely
eliminating a set of activities or parts of the organizational structure. In
others, it might mean scaling back or divesting them, that is, handing them
over to another organization to manage. Cutback decisions require developing a thorough understanding of why a structure, process, or program is no
longer appropriate and how and to what extent it should be curtailed.

This chapter begins with a brief overview of the conditions that lead to
cutbacks. This is followed by a discussion of the organizational dynamics
that often accompany them. A cutback matrix is provided, with a discussion

of each of the due diligence criteria for cutbacks. The chapter concludes with two illustrative minicases.

Dimensions of Cutting Back

> *Loss is nothing else but change, and change is nature's delight.*
>
> —Marcus Aurelius Antoninus

When managers talk about cutting back, they use a number of terms: *downsize, right-size, RIF (reduction in force), downscale, scale back, economize,* and *rationalize.* These are often used interchangeably to refer to reducing the size of an organization. However, each means something slightly different and emphasizes different dimensions of the cutback decision.

First, *downsizing* has been used in both the commercial and nonprofit sectors to mean reducing the size of a business or organization, especially by cutting the workforce. *Right-sizing* is a euphemism found in the business press meaning the same thing. The term is an attempt to make a difficult process more palatable. *RIF*—an acronym for *reduction in force*—is primarily used by government to describe the employee layoffs that result from budget cuts. In these situations, the emphasis is on cutting back the human resource base of the organization to realize cost savings.

Second, *downscaling* or *scaling back* refers to decreasing the relative size of the organization. It is used to describe a cutback situation where an organization's operations or programs are reduced in a holistic and balanced way. There is a reduction in both human resources and related financial and material resources. Reducing the number of satellite offices, the number of performances, or the number of programs are examples of downscaling or scaling back.

Third, *economize* and *rationalize* emphasize the financial dimension. The focus is on reducing expenditures or eliminating waste. This type of cutting back is usually associated with a reduction in or loss of funding, the desire to balance an annual budget, or efforts to stem a growing deficit. Many managers have received directives to economize that require them to cut their budgets by a fixed percentage or amount.

No matter where the emphasis falls, trends in the environment set the stage for periodic organizational contraction. Cutbacks happen when there is no longer adequate need or support for a particular program or activity. For example, in some communities, the increased number of nonprofits has created a redundancy in programming and with it increased competition for limited funds. Also, cutbacks are part of the transition when a new way of doing things comes along that makes old approaches obsolete. Established systems are abandoned to make way for the new. Nearly all nonprofits have experienced this shift in resources as they upgrade electronic media and computer technology.

No matter what they're called or where the emphasis is, cutback decisions are often made in a reactive way, with action taken quickly when a problem emerges. For example, if a deficit is projected, management might immediately move to eliminate or scale back programs. Short-term financial stability indeed results, but community relationships and staff confidence might be seriously undermined in the process. Unless the decision is fully informed and communicated to the relevant internal and external stakeholders, the cutback can have an immediate destabilizing effect. Also, reactively approaching a critical cutback without understanding its implications for the future can perpetuate a climate of uncertainty.

The emotional dimension of cutback decisions should not be underestimated. We've discussed how new ideas leading to organizational growth are often emotionally charged—but in a positive way, as a novel idea with all its promise can be exciting. In the feasibility, pilot, and implementation stages, the decision makers temper this enthusiasm for change through the due diligence process to make better choices.

Emotions run high in cutback situations too, but these feelings are different. What kind of person would be eager to lay off coworkers or eliminate services needed in the community? Instead of enthusiasm, the organization is dealing with fear. A climate of apprehension surrounds most cutback decisions. Those who rely on the organization are confronted with a potential loss, sometimes anticipating that the nonprofit is going to abandon the community. Internal stakeholders (staff and volunteers) can have a number of concerns, ranging from anxiety about a change of routine, to having fewer resources to work with, to losing their jobs.

For cutbacks to be effective and managed well, they must be viewed as part of a broader retrenchment plan. Too often *retrenchment* is used interchangeably for *downsize, economize,* or one of the other terms associated with cutbacks. However, looking at the original military meaning of the term shows it can be an important strategic option. *Retrenchment* means to fall back, dig in, reorganize, and rethink in ways that will position the group to move forward in the future. Failure to consider the long-term consequences of a cutback, both positive and negative, is to discount its potential impact on the organization. Indeed, when an organization eliminates something, it is usually freeing up resources that can be put to better use. Cuts are tactics that, as part of a broader retrenchment strategy, can reorder resources to support the organization's mission. Without an understanding of how the resources should be redeployed, the cutback is not fully planned, let alone strategic. Using the due diligence process lets the nonprofit approach cutback decisions from this strategic perspective.

The Cutback Matrix

> *Remember! Things in life will not always run smoothly. Sometimes we will be rising toward the heights—then all will seem to reverse itself and start downward.*
>
> *—Endicott Peabody*

The cutback matrix in Exhibit 8.1 is identical to the feasibility matrix. But instead of being used to assess an idea that has not yet been put into practice, it is used to reassess an idea that has been implemented and been in place for some time. In scoring the matrix, the decision makers critically examine if and to what extent the portion of the organization they are evaluating continues to meet the due diligence criteria. They revisit the critical factors that indicate whether the idea continues to be feasible or practical. Cutback decisions are supported by evidence that shows considerable risk, inadequate leverage, or problems sustaining what is currently in place. The lower the scores are, the more likely a cutback decision will result. The specific questions that guide the discussion of each of the due diligence criteria help the decision makers understand the degree to which an existing structure, process, or program is no longer viable. In assigning weights to the criteria, the appropriate individuals reflect what is strategically important to that specific organization.

Exhibit 8.1. Sample Individual Cutback Matrix.			
Criteria	*Weight*	*Decision Maker Score*	*Weighted Score*
Strategic alignment			
Feasibility			
Expertise			
Reasonable cost			
Fit			
Measurable impact			
Appropriate scope			
Personnel			
Practicality			
Measurable productivity			
Risk factors			
Collaboration			
Broader benefit			
Financial health			
Organization development			
Board oversight			
Totals	**100**		
Total possible weighted score			**1,000**
Percentage agreement			**%**

A set of questions for each of the criteria that guide the cutback scoring follows. Again, these are similar to feasibility criteria, but they are intended to help assess ongoing feasibility and practicality.

Strategic Alignment

If a structure, process, or program no longer meets or supports the organization's strategy, it is by definition obsolete. Sometimes obsolescence is a matter of degree, as when a program supports the strategy only marginally or partially supports a low-priority item.

Questions to Ask to Assess Strategic Alignment

☑ To what extent does this structure, program, or process support the organization's current role in the community and reflect its values, vision, mission, and goals?

☑ Does this activity continue to fit within the organization's existing strategic and operating plans? Which specific goals does it support? How specifically does it support them?

☑ What is the demonstrated strategic impact of the part of the organization under review? That is, has it significantly enhanced the organization's ability to pursue major high-priority action items and benefited the organization overall? Or has it only marginally contributed to minor, low-priority items that affect solely specific programs or departments?

Once the decision makers understand in detail to what degree the item under review no longer supports the organization's strategy, they assign a weight. The more misaligned or the poorer the strategic fit is, the lower the score. For example, a program that does not meet any of the organization's strategic priorities will score a 0.

Feasibility

In some cases, comparable programs or practices might have already been evaluated and eliminated in other organizations. Similar organizations often face similar programmatic and administrative issues. Some organizations hold on to practices that have been demonstrated to be obsolete and eliminated by other organizations. There is a greater likelihood that stakeholders will accept a cutback if other organizations have already successfully abandoned similar ideas. The decision makers should research the proposed cuts to learn how other organizations have addressed them.

Question to Ask to Assess Feasibility

☑ Has any other nonprofit made this kind of cutback before? If the answer is no, the decision makers should ask, "Why not?" If the answer is yes, a more detailed study of the features and benefits of the cutback in other organizations should follow. In particular, the decision makers should look at the organization's similarities and differences that might support or undermine the process in their own organization.

The more examples there are of similar successful cutbacks, the lower the decision makers' scores will be.

Expertise

Sustainability is linked to maintaining relevant knowledge or a skill set in the organization. Assessing whether the organization still has access to the appropriate expertise is another important factor in determining the viability of an idea. In some cases, the organization may no longer have the in-house expertise a program needs. For example, when dealing with information technology, small organizations can often acquire systems that are beyond the know-how of anyone on the staff. As a result, they do not use the system to its full capacity and are constantly dependent on external consultants.

Questions to Ask to Assess Expertise

☑ What type of specialized expertise was and is necessary to implement and sustain this idea? A detailed inventory of the knowledge or skills needed should be developed.

☑ Does this expertise currently reside within the organization? That is, do current staff members have the expertise to sustain implementation at the appropriate level? If they do not, the decision makers should see if it is being sourced from outside the organization.

☑ If the expertise was obtained from outside the organization, where did it come from? The decision makers should determine how appropriate and stable the external sources have been.

☑ If the expertise was originally obtained from outside the organization, was there an insufficient transfer of knowledge to the organization? If necessary, has the organization maintained an ongoing relationship with an external provider? Examine in detail the contracting arrangements, the costs, and how the relationship is managed.

The less expertise is available to the organization, the lower the decision makers' scores will be.

Reasonable Cost

It is critical to know how much it costs to sustain the activity. If the initial budgets for the innovation were inadequate, it is often only after implementation that the financial strain becomes apparent. The decision makers need a comprehensive analysis of the full range of costs needed to sustain the program, along with future budget projections that accompany any proposed cuts.

Questions to Ask to Assess Cost

☑ What are the full costs for sustaining this structure, process, or program? A budget should be developed that includes direct and indirect costs, fixed and variable costs, and sunk versus relevant costs. A clearly detailed narrative should accompany the budget detailing the reasoning supporting each line. How does this compare with what has actually been budgeted for implementation?

☑ Have the budgets for implementation been realistic? The decision makers should review the assumptions made about the costs in each budget line.

☑ Where have the resources used to support implementation been coming from? Problem areas are often supported at the expense of other organizational activities. For example, a reserve fund might be depleted to support an activity that has not been budgeted appropriately.

The more disproportionate the activity's costs are to the overall budget, the lower the decision makers' scores will be.

Fit

The decision makers must review the impact on the organization internally and externally. This includes assessing both positive and negative implementation effects on existing programs and operations. In addition, fit with the plans and activities of the broader nonprofit community should be reviewed.

In the case of internal structures or operations, misfit will stress the organization. Problems in scheduling, inappropriate staff assignments, or conflicting processes and programs have a negative effect on performance. In addition, what has been implemented might be at odds with the expectations of the organization's client base, in conflict or in competition with the work of other nonprofits, or misaligned with funder interests and priorities.

Questions to Ask to Assess Fit

☑ Does the program fit within the organization's annual operating plans? In addition to overall strategic alignment, review the specific program, department, and administrative goals. Which staff and volunteers have been involved, and how does their involvement affect their overall workload? How has implementation affected the allocation of other resources, such as space and equipment?

☑ How has implementation affected the community? Find out exactly how it has or has not met client needs and expectations. Also review the fit within the nonprofit community, looking for redundancy or conflict. Assess the available funding opportunities to determine whether there has been or will be sufficient interest and support.

The poorer the fit is with internal operations and external stakeholders, the lower the decision makers' scores will be.

Measurable Impact

Measurement is critical to assess whether the activity has been effective and to what degree. If the impact of implementation has not been or cannot be measured, there is no way to know whether it is supporting the organization's mission or undermining it. In other cases, there might be good measures in place, but evaluations indicate the impact is well below what is expected.

In general, when there is no monitoring system in place or the monitoring system indicates poor performance, it is a signal that corrective changes should be made.

Questions to Ask to Assess Impact

☑ What specific positive change was implementation intended to bring about? What were the actual results? The level of impact should also be compared against any standards established for reasonable performance.

☑ How was the impact to be measured? Assess the validity and reliability of the indicators. Look at how the monitoring was carried out. If there have been problems with the measures or the process of measuring, the information collected about impact is flawed.

The less impact there has been or the less reliable the measures are, the lower the decision makers' scores will be.

Appropriate Scope

Some activities overwhelm an organization's management and resource capacity, if the nonprofit does not have the experience, infrastructure, and resource base to sustain it adequately.

Review of the earlier criteria, especially cost and fit, helps to determine whether the scope of the implementation was appropriate and continues to be, or whether it places too great a burden on the organization's resources and its stakeholders.

Question to Ask to Assess Scope

☑ Have the resources budgeted for implementation been disproportionate to the operating budget of the organization? The decision makers should review the amount budgeted for the activity versus the annual operating budget and examine any changes in either that have occurred during the course of implementation.

The greater the amount budgeted to an activity, the greater the likelihood of inappropriate scope is. The less appropriate the scope is, the lower the decision makers' scores will be.

Personnel

Over the course of implementation, staff members might not have the appropriate knowledge, experience, and professional skills to support it. Sometimes this is the result of normal staff turnover.

Questions to Ask to Assess Personnel

- ☑ Has the organization had the appropriate personnel to sustain implementation? Does it currently? Specific staff skill sets should be reviewed.

- ☑ Has the organization had the appropriate personnel to manage the activity? Does it currently? Has management been able to coordinate implementation with the organization's operations on an ongoing basis, as well as manage external stakeholders?

The less qualified the personnel are, the lower the decision makers' scores will be.

Practicality

Over time, conditions might change so that it is no longer practical—that is, sensible or useful—to continue implementation. Another organization in the community might have developed a better competing project, for example, or funding might be lost, or the organization might have more pressing priorities.

Acknowledging that something is impractical often requires acknowledging that it has produced negative consequences. This can be difficult for people who are heavily invested in the activity. In evaluating practicality, all of the previous eight factors must be discussed and balanced to understand exactly what is at stake if the organization continues to implement the activity.

Question to Ask to Assess Practicality

☑ Should we sustain what has been put in place at this time? Review the previous criteria, and if they have all received low scores, the activity is most likely impractical.

The less practical implementation is, the lower the decision makers' scores will be.

Measurable Productivity

The decision makers should review any productivity gains resulting from implementation. That is, they should examine how much return was realized from the effort and resources invested. Ideally, implementation should not only have its desired impact but should also increase overall operating efficiency. In other words, the organization should have been able to do more with what it has.

Once again, measurement is critical to determining viability. Productivity is calculated by dividing the results obtained by the resources expended. If there has been no reliable measure of impact or little understanding of the costs during the course of implementation, productivity is at best questionable. If sound measures have been used to assess efficiency over the course of implementation, the numbers should show whether productivity has been enhanced, increased only marginally, or diminished.

Questions to Ask to Assess Productivity

☑ Has implementation had a measurable impact on the productivity of the organization? If so, has it been positive or negative?

☑ If productivity has increased, has it been offset by a decrease in productivity in another area?

If there are no productivity measures or if productivity is low, the decision makers' scores will be low.

Risk Factors

Implementation might have exposed the organization to risks resulting in damage or loss. In these cases, decision makers determine what has gone wrong and what might go wrong in the future, and they examine how the organization managed any problems.

Several common types of risk can damage the organization and its relationships: technological, personnel, and financial. The key to assessing viability is to identify the specific risks associated with implementing the idea, examine how these risks have been managed, and consider how they might be managed in the future.

Question to Ask to Assess Risk

☑ Have the risks associated with implementation resulted in damage or loss? Pay specific attention to technological, personnel, funding, and market risks. In addition, review the systems used to manage the risk and determine whether they are adequate or can be improved.

The larger the number of risks identified, the greater the amount of damage or loss sustained or anticipated, and the less able the organization has been to manage the risks, the lower the decision makers' scores will be.

Collaboration

Implementation sometimes relies on collaborative efforts with other organizations. Lack of planning, incompatible organizational cultures, and unclear roles can undermine efforts to work together. In some situations, the collaborative relationships themselves are the issue. In others, there is no partner that can adequately share the risk and contribute resources and expertise.

Question to Ask to Assess Collaboration

☑ Has implementation been sustained by more than one organization, and should it be? If so, identify the organizations, and assess the benefits and problems.

The fewer the number of viable collaborators there are, the lower the decision makers' scores will be.

Broader Benefit

Sometimes the benefits of implementation go beyond the organizations directly involved. A sustainable idea can serve as a model for other nonprofits.

Questions to Ask to Assess Broader Benefit

☑ Have the benefits of implementation extended beyond the organizations directly involved? As with collaboration, specific organizations should be examined to determine how they have and have not benefited.

☑ Have the benefits been disseminated? That is, were dissemination plans developed and carried out? The decision makers should also determine if any other organizations adopted the new idea and benefited from it.

The fewer the organizations that have benefited, the lower the decision makers' scores will be.

Financial Health

Ideally, implementation should strengthen the financial health of the organization and support its ability to generate revenue, earned and unearned.

Question to Ask to Assess Financial Health

☑ Has the activity contributed to the financial health of the organization? The decision makers should review the costs and revenues associated with the activity over time. The more precise the understanding of the impact on the financials is, the better the assessment will be.

The fewer the financial benefits there are, the lower the decision makers' scores will be.

Organization Development

In addition to contributing to the overall financial health of the organization, implementation should have contributed to the growth and development of the organization, positioning it to do more and better work.

Question to Ask to Assess Organization Development

☑ Has implementation contributed to the development of the organization's program, staff, and administrative capacity? Programs should have enhanced content, quality, or reach. Ideally, there should be evidence that staff skill sets have expanded and that employees are better able to meet their personal and professional goals. In the case of administrative capacity, implementation should contribute to making work processes more efficient and effective.

The less that implementation contributes to developing program, staff, and administrative capacity, the lower the decision makers' scores will be.

Board Oversight

If implementation does not have the appropriate board oversight, the critical element in the monitoring and accountability process is missing at the strategic level. In addition, if board members are directly involved in implementation without a set of checks and balances, potential conflicts of interest can result.

Questions to Ask to Assess Board Oversight

- ☑ Has the board had the appropriate structures, processes, and policies in place to oversee implementation? Has it been accommodated within standard board priorities, policies, and ongoing committee work?

- ☑ Have board members been directly involved in implementation, and has this complemented or conflicted with their oversight roles? Have the appropriate checks and balances been in place?

The less involved the board has been with appropriate oversight, the lower the decision makers' scores will be.

The minicases that follow provide examples of organizations faced with cutback decisions. The first is a situation where a new executive director uses the matrix to distance the decision from an emotional attachment to past practices. The second provides an example of how the due diligence process and matrix can be used by a management team deciding which of several successful programs must be cut because of a loss of funding.

THE CASE OF THE EAST SIDE CLINIC

The advantage of the emotions is that they lead us astray.
—*Oscar Wilde*, **The Picture of Dorian Gray**

The East Side Clinic provides a range of health services for the local community. Its philosophy is holistic and is reflected in its range of programming and partnerships. The clinic provides basic medical care and health education programs on-site. It brings in additional services by working closely with other health care providers. These include the visiting nurse association, a local nutrition program, and the community mental health group.

Mr. Baxter, the new executive director, was reviewing the budget for the upcoming year, when he realized there would be a $100,000 shortfall on its annual $3 million budget. After several discussions with the board chair and finance committee, as well as the clinic's chief financial officer, he realized the only way to balance the budget was to make cuts.

When he had reviewed the programming and administration, Mr. Baxter found only two possible cuts that would make up the difference. One is the fair that the clinic hosts every year in its local neighborhood. The event is popular and always gets good press and generates goodwill. Although there are some health-related activities like blood pressure screening, it is basically a traditional street fair with vendors and entertainment. The cost of the fair is $150,000. The other possible cut is the position of full-time psychiatric nurse staffing an off-site outreach program for the homeless. The cost of the position with benefits is almost exactly $100,000.

Mr. Baxter proceeds with the due diligence process so that he can compare the options. First, he scores the matrix based on the clinic's priorities. Then he scores each of the two possible cuts independently and compares the results. His assessment follows.

Option 1: Eliminate the Fair

Strategic alignment. Mr. Baxter reviews the origins of the fair and the range of its activities. It had its roots in the clinic's opening-day event thirty years before and was staffed by a group of committed volunteers. It was originally intended to acquaint the neighborhood with the services offered at the clinic and to create a sense of ownership in the local community. In subsequent decades, the event grew considerably and became a community celebration with food, games, music, and all the activities associated with a party. Health-related activities were relegated to a few small tables by the entrance to the clinic's building. The clinic staff now plays the major role in running the event, with negligible volunteer support. The clinic is the sole sponsor of the event. The clinic's mission is to provide access to quality health care in the community. Mr. Baxter finds that the event complements the strategy in only a marginal way. Score: 1.

Feasibility. In discussions with colleagues in the region, Mr. Baxter learns that several clinics participate in similar events hosted by local hospitals. They do not themselves host the events, however, since they are too costly and labor intensive. Instead, they set up a booth or table in the hospital event and supply literature and simple medical screenings. Score: 0.

Expertise. The staff, most of whom have medical or administrative backgrounds, handle all aspects of the fair. With the exception of one junior development associate, no one has any professional experience in planning or managing special events. Score: 1.

Reasonable cost. As Mr. Baxter reviews the costs associated with recent fairs, he realizes that there has been little budgeting for the event. The same vendors have been contracted year after year with no competitive bidding process. As a result, the cost of the fair has increased considerably over the years. Score: 0.

Fit. Although the fair builds a sense of community and provides limited wellness education, the event is not designed with the health care needs of the community as its focus. Moreover, none of the clinic's partnering organizations participate in the event because their management strongly feels that it is not a good use of their staff and resources. Finally, the clinic's development office has tried to develop funder or sponsorship support for the event, but with no success. Score: 1.

Measurable impact. The impact of the fair on the overall health of the community has never been considered, let alone measured. The only indicators of impact are a few newspaper clippings kept by the development office that provide anecdotal testimonials about the event. Score: 0.

Appropriate scope. Mr. Baxter reviews the time sheets of the employees for the month prior to the fair. He realizes that a full 25 percent of the staff's time across the board is devoted to preparing for the fair. In the three months before that, it is approximately 10 percent. Based on these realities, Mr. Baxter calculates the cost in staff time to be $110,000. This is in addition to the direct costs of $150,000. Together they bring the budget for the event to $260,000, over 8 percent of the clinic's annual budget. Score: 0.

Personnel. The current staff, including the clinical professionals, devote a major portion of their available time to setting up for the special event. This takes time away from their primary responsibilities. And as previously mentioned, with the exception of one development staff member, none have been trained in special event planning or management. Mr. Baxter feels that this is not an appropriate use of the current staff's skills. Score: 0.

Practicality. Given the pressing health care issues facing the community, such as childhood asthma and a high infant mortality rate, the demands on the clinic are anticipated to grow. Mr. Baxter considers any activity that does not address any of the community's health issues impractical at this time. Score: 0.

Measurable productivity. Given the increasing costs over time, Mr. Baxter determines that the productivity related to the event is decreasing. Also, the productivity of the staff in their regular work is diminished by their work on the fair. Score: 0.

Risk factors. The fair raises two risk factors. First, Mr. Baxter realizes that there has been no insurance coverage for the event. If anything were to happen during the fair, the organization and board would be liable. Second, the fair puts a significant financial strain on the organization and will most likely continue to do so. Score: 0.

Collaboration. No other nonprofits participate in the fair. It has no corporate, foundation, or individual sponsors. Score: 0.

Broader benefit. The fair has not served as a model for other nonprofits. Score: 0.

Financial health. Because the fair is supported by the clinic's operating funds, it limits the organization's flexibility. Moreover, the clinic's deficit can be closely tied to the costs of the fair. Score: 0.

Organization development. Staff and board members have argued that the fair positions the clinic in the community in such a way that more people will use its services. No objective data, however, support this assertion. In addition, there might be significant opportunities lost to promote health care offered at the clinic when staff and resources are devoted to non-health-related activities. Score: 1.

Board oversight. Some local board members attend the fair every year. However, there is no direct formal committee oversight of the event, and no formal policies apply to it. The lack of insurance coverage underscores the lack of connection with the board and its fiduciary role. Score: 0.

Option 2: Eliminate the Psychiatric Nursing Position

Strategic alignment. The clinic's mission is to provide access to quality health care in the community. The growing number of homeless in the community has been a major concern. They are among the community's most vulnerable citizens. The psychiatric nurse position was developed because many homeless are mentally ill and will not come to the clinic. The nurse holds regular hours at the shelters and other locations where the homeless receive services. Mr. Baxter finds the position closely aligned with the mission and holistic philosophy of the clinic, as well as with several of the high-priority action items in the strategic plan. Score: 10.

Feasibility. Many clinics and community mental health centers use an outreach approach with homeless clients. It is well documented that this population does not use centralized services, but they do seek services at mobile units and satellite programs at human service sites. Score: 10.

Expertise. The psychiatric nurse has the necessary expertise to address both the mental and physical health needs of homeless clients. In addition, she is able to collect data and carry out research about the general health of the homeless population in the community. Score: 10.

Reasonable cost. The position with benefits and travel allowance costs the clinic approximately $100,000. This is in line with the local labor market. Score: 10.

Fit. Because of a shrinking economy, homelessness is a growing problem in the Eastside community. The clinic is the primary source of health care for this population. The local government and network of human services agencies serving Eastside have made addressing the issue of homelessness a priority. Several major funders have pledged multiyear support for the effort. The psychiatric nurse position is primarily funded through a multiyear renewable grant. The effort is in its second year of a three-year cycle. Score: 10.

Measurable impact. A comprehensive evaluation plan and assessment process were developed as part of the grant application for funds to support the psychiatric nurse position. These incorporate a set of standard utilization and health measures. The psychiatric nurse routinely collects and assesses the appropriate data. The impact has been significant: an increasing number of homeless people are seeking out health services. In addition to mental health problems, the nurse has been able to perform routine blood work, administer flu shots, and refer individuals to other service providers for nutrition support and maternity care. Score: 10.

Appropriate scope. The scope of the activity is very small relative to the clinic's overall budget. Because the work is housed off-site, there is little stress on the organization's resource base. Score: 10.

Personnel. The program is staffed by an experienced psychiatric nurse with expertise in working with homeless populations. Score: 10.

Practicality. Given the growing homeless population, their health care needs, the issues of access, and the availability of foundation support, Mr. Baxter believes that the position is practical. Score: 10.

Measurable productivity. The cost of the outreach program is fixed for the three-year term of the grant. During the first year, the number of people who were treated grew steadily. Measurable productivity is increasing. Score: 10.

Risk factors. Mr. Baxter thinks the risk factors are minimal. There is some technological risk. The nurse tabulates data on a laptop that she carries from site to site. If the laptop malfunctions or is lost, data can be lost. However, a strict backup protocol is followed every day to manage this risk. There is also the possibility that the nurse will leave the position, which would cause a disruption in service. However, sufficient psychiatric nurses are available in the local labor market to fill the vacant position. Because the position is tied to grant funding, there is the financial risk that the grant will not be renewed. However, the program has met the goals set out in the original grant proposal, so renewal is more likely. In addition, the development department is in discussion with other funders who are also supporting the local effort to address issues facing the homeless. Finally—and unfortunately—the homeless population is growing, ensuring a continued market for the program. Score: 10.

Collaboration. The clinic participates with numerous local nonprofits in providing sites and through referral relationships: two local homeless shelters, the Salvation Army, a church, the community mental health center, the maternity care center, and the local hospital. Score: 10.

Broader benefit. The report of the first year's findings was disseminated to local nonprofits and funders who address the issue of homelessness. Two pieces of information were obtained that should increase the ability of these groups to serve the homeless population. First, the average age of the homeless population is significantly younger than originally assumed: thirty-two, as opposed to forty. Second, there is a growing number of homeless families. Many current programs are targeted to single men in their early forties. This information will make it possible for agencies to adapt their services to this population. Score: 10.

Financial health. Because the psychiatric nurse position is supported in whole by grant funds, it poses no financial stress on the organization. However, if external funding cannot be secured in the future, the clinic will have to support it from operating funds, and that would most likely create a deficit. Score: 6.

Organization development. Mr. Baxter sees the psychiatric nurse position as a possible step in making the clinic more responsive to the Eastside community. To date, it has been a significant outreach effort that has forged partnerships with key nonprofits, and it has informed local policy discussion about the issue of homelessness. The effort can position the organization for growth through similar collaborative efforts in the future. Score: 10.

Board oversight. Because the position is tied to the organization's strategic priorities, the board systematically reviews the outreach program in relationship to the clinic's plans. Score: 10.

Mr. Baxter will recommend that the annual fair be eliminated and the psychiatric nurse retained. Although there is significant emotional investment in the fair, the argument for serving the homeless is overwhelming: in the matrix analysis, the fair scored 4 percent agreement, while the nursing position scored an overwhelming 99 percent. In terms of the clinic's identity and role in the Eastside community, the relatively low-profile visiting nurse does more to advance the organization than a large public celebration does. Mr. Baxter uses the matrix in Exhibit 8.2 in his presentations to board and staff to walk them through the key issues and his reasoning objectively.

Exhibit 8.2. Summary of Mr. Baxter's Weighting and Scores

Criteria	Weight	Option 1: Eliminate the Fair	Option 1 Weighted Score	Option 2: Eliminate the Nurse Position	Option 2 Weighted Score
Strategic alignment	18	1	18	10	180
Feasibility	14	0	0	10	140
Expertise	10	1	10	10	100
Reasonable cost	10	0	0	10	100
Fit	10	1	10	10	100
Measurable impact	8	0	0	10	80
Appropriate scope	5	0	0	10	50
Personnel	4	0	0	10	40
Practicality	4	0	0	10	40
Measurable productivity	4	0	0	10	40
Risk factors	4	0	0	10	40
Collaboration	2	0	0	10	20
Broader benefit	2	0	0	10	20
Financial health	2	0	0	6	12
Organization development	2	1	2	10	20
Board oversight	1	0	0	10	10
Totals	**100**	**4**	**40**	**156**	**992**
Total possible weighted score			**1,000**		**1,000**
Percentage agreement			**4%**		**99%**

THE CASE OF THE UNIVERSITY SATELLITES

My mother buried three husbands—and two of them were just napping.

—Rita Rudner

Dean Johnson heads up the School of Business and Public Administration at Southeastern University, a midsized regional institution. The school is at the end of a ten-year period of growth during which enrollments increased, innovative programs were developed, new faculty were hired, and facilities were expanded. However, projections for the coming year indicate that the school is now facing the beginning of a challenging period: the region is experiencing a downturn in the economy, several major employers are leaving the area, and the population is declining rather than growing. At the same time, the number of higher education programs in professional education available to students in the area is increasing, including a new branch campus of a major state university with subsidized tuition as well as numerous accredited online programs.

Dean Johnson has reviewed the budget projections for the next year and anticipates a significant drop in student enrollment, especially in the continuing education programs. She attributes this downward trend to increased competition from other institutions, coupled with the fact that there are fewer employee reimbursement plans for professional development as companies leave the area. There is nothing the school can do to reverse this trend, so the dean must make cuts to balance the budget for the coming year.

During the course of the school's expansion, three satellite facilities for continuing education were established to create a greater presence in the region, as well as to make attending programs more convenient for students. All were developed on the same model and are located in rental space built out with classrooms, laboratories, meeting rooms, and offices. One is in a new suburban office park right off a major highway. Another is in an old high school building in a densely populated residential area. The third is in a high-rise office building in the downtown business district of the region's largest city. All cost approximately the same amount to operate annually. Eliminating any one of them would balance the budget.

After consulting with the senior administration and her own management team, which includes program heads and academic department chairs, Dean Johnson decides one of the satellites must be closed. But the question is, Which one? Of course—like the rest of the sagacious decision makers in this book—Dean Johnson is familiar with the matrix, so she decides to use it to compare the three alternatives. Based on her discussions with the university and school leadership, she assigns weights to each of the decision criteria. Given the circumstances, strategic alignment and budgetary considerations are the most heavily weighted factors. Impact is heavily weighted too, as Dean Johnson hopes to do as little damage as possible to the relationship with the community and students that the satellites have helped build.

The summary of Dean Johnson's weighting and scoring is presented in Exhibit 8.3. The scores are closer than those in the East Side Clinic case: 58 percent for the satellite in the office park, 77 percent for the one in the neighborhood, and 73 percent for the downtown location. Clearly they are similar options and vary significantly only on three dimensions: fit, practicality, and risk factors. Dean Johnson's careful analysis reveals that the satellite in the office park is the likely candidate for cutback, for three reasons. First, several of the nearby businesses that have sent employees to that site for training will be downsizing in the next six months, creating a problem with fit. Second, the state university has recently located a branch campus within a mile of the office park. The satellite was built knowing this, but the competitive threat was largely ignored. Many of the programs at the satellite cannot compete with similar subsidized programs offered by the state university. In retrospect, the decision to locate the satellite in the office park near a competitor was impractical, and it still is. Third, the lease on the office park site expires in the next year. Negotiations have begun with the owner, who is asking for a much higher rent in hopes of offsetting his losses from any downsizing commercial tenants. Understanding these differences, Dean Johnson is comfortable with the decision to close the office park site.

Exhibit 8.3. Dean Johnson's Weighted Scoring and Percentage Agreement of Each Cutback Option.

Criteria	Weight	Office Park	Weighted	Neighborhood	Weighted	Downtown	Weighted
Strategic alignment	10	10	100	10	100	10	100
Feasibility	8	5	40	5	40	5	40
Expertise	2	2	4	2	4	2	4
Reasonable cost	10	8	80	9	90	8	80
Fit	8	6	48	9	72	9	72
Measurable impact	10	7	70	8	80	8	80
Appropriate scope	8	8	64	9	72	8	64
Personnel	4	2	8	2	8	3	12
Practicality	10	5	50	9	90	9	90
Measurable productivity	2	3	6	3	6	3	6
Risk factors	10	3	30	9	90	9	90
Collaboration	2	0	0	0	0	0	0
Broader benefit	4	2	8	5	20	2	8
Financial health	10	7	70	9	90	8	80
Organization development	1	5	5	5	5	5	5
Board oversight	1	1	1	1	1	1	1
Totals	**100**	**74**	**584**	**95**	**768**	**90**	**732**
Percentage agreement			**58%**		**77%**		**73%**

9

Putting the Matrix to Work

We shall not fail or falter; we shall not weaken or tire ...
Give us the tools and we will finish the job.

—Sir Winston Churchill

AT THIS POINT, you should have a basic understanding of the five elements in critical decision making:

1. The different types of decisions and how most people generally approach them successfully

2. The problems inherent in addressing critical choices that pose significant potential risks and rewards

3. The due diligence process that investors use for making complex decisions in business settings

4. The application of the due diligence process in nonprofit settings to evaluate critical decisions

5. The use of the matrix tool to support the process

You are now ready to put the matrix to work. We could end the book right here and wish you good luck, but there is one additional thing we want to tell you: how people in specific nonprofit jobs can use the matrix. The method is general, but depending on their positions, people use it for various purposes. Board members, executive directors, department and program managers, funders, and consultants can all use the matrix for making critical decisions but in different situations. This chapter offers a brief overview of how each group can put the matrix to use.

Boards of Directors

If the bloodbath must come, let's get on with it.

—*Governor Ronald Reagan to the University of California Board of Regents*

Board members have the job of making strategy and policy decisions. Usually they make them as part of the nonprofit's routine planning and budgeting activities. However, major opportunities and challenges often disrupt the normal work flow of the board. These are the events that can lead to major changes for the organization in terms of its mission, role in the community, structure, or resources. They are usually accompanied by a flurry of telephone calls, emergency meetings, and the deployment of ad hoc committees or task force groups. If you've served on a board, you've probably had this experience of making a critical decision.

If we try to inventory all the significant novel decisions that a board might face, we would have to write another book. Instead, we offer some representative categories that should be familiar to most of our readers. If you haven't lived through them yourself, our guess is you know an organization and board that has.

The Building Opportunity

In the best of all possible worlds, building projects are the result of careful study of the organization's and community's needs and the financial feasibility of acquiring, maintaining, and operating a new facility. But of course we don't inhabit the best of all possible worlds; we inhabit this one, where on any given day a building opportunity might emerge. Here are some examples that we have encountered in our work with nonprofits that have resulted in full-blown, unplanned capital projects:

- A "For Sale" sign appears one day on the building next door.
- Someone calls and offers to give the organization a building.

- A board member visits a similar organization in another city, falls in love with its new facility, and proposes to build a similar one.

- Another nonprofit in the community moves and leaves behind a building that seems desirable to similar organizations.

All of these cases raise considerable risk and potentially major long-term resource requirements.

The Windfall Bequest

These do actually happen. Occasionally nonprofits are included in wills—sometimes without being informed—and the size of the bequest can be significant. If the funds are restricted, the board either accepts the gift with its terms or turns it down. For bequests that are large and unrestricted, the board must develop guidelines for allocating the new resources.

Sometimes the gift is so large it can dwarf the organization's current resource base—the organizational equivalent of an average person winning the lottery. This is a rare occurrence, but when it does happen, it can force the organization to redesign itself and shift its mission in a relatively short period of time. The recent well-known case of the Kroc bequest to the Salvation Army serves as an example. The bequest of $1.5 billion is restricted to building community centers. In accepting this bequest, the Salvation Army is significantly shifting other resources to program and operate the new Kroc Centers.

In cases where there are no restrictions on the bequest, allocating the new money becomes the issue. Should the organization retire its current debts? Should it expand existing programs or develop new ones? Should the staff get raises? And what about that new building? And so it goes, as staff, board, and constituents advocate for a pet project. Without a clear process to guide the decision, it can become political, and the eventual outcome will be less than optimal.

The Proposed Merger

Nonprofits are sometimes approached by other organizations with the idea of combining resources. Sometimes the proposal is limited to specific activities and might include sharing facilities, specialized staff, or information. At other times, full mergers are suggested that will result in a single new organization.

When a nonprofit is considering a full merger, board members from all the potential merger organizations become involved in the decision.

The idea might originate with one of the organizations that will eventually be a part of the merged entity. In some cases, a struggling organization might see merger with a more stable organization as an alternative to dissolution. Or a stable organization might view taking on a struggling organization as a way to grow. In other cases, mergers might be initiated by funders with the intention of eliminating redundant organizations, reducing overhead, and creating more efficient organizations. They sometimes provide financial incentives to support the merger.

Board members ultimately make the decision of whether to merge. Whenever two or more organizations come together, they bring with them all of their strengths and weaknesses. A method for assessing the potential risks and benefits is key to making a sound choice.

Using the Matrix

When the board is brought in, the decision is critical and will significantly alter the course of the nonprofit's future. The matrix tool can organize and present the data in a way that is helpful to all board members. It can also be used to record and track each board member's opinions as the decision is studied and discussed. And once a decision is reached, the information collected using the matrix can be presented to staff and external constituents.

Executive Directors

> *Bullwinkle: You just leave that to my pal. He's the brains of the outfit.*
> *General: What does that make you?*
> *Bullwinkle: What else? An executive.*
>
> —*Jay Ward*

There's more truth in what Bullwinkle says than most of us care to admit. Nonprofit executive directors are adept at using other people's brainpower. It's how they get their work done. They rely on board members, staff, and a range of constituents and stakeholders to provide them with the detailed information they need to manage effectively. And when it comes to making critical decisions, they base their choices largely on what they learn from others.

This is not to say that executive directors are brainless. Most executives do have sophisticated knowledge about a substantive aspect of their work. For example, they might have started their nonprofit careers in the direct delivery of service or programming as social workers, classroom teachers, medical doctors, or actors. Others might have begun in specialized administrative positions as development staff, certified public accountants, human resource specialists, or facilities managers. However, as their careers progressed, they assumed more and more managerial responsibility for organizational processes. Their work increasingly focused on coordinating the work of others, whether that work was tied to program or administrative activities. Once nonprofit managers rise to the position of executive director, their job consists of overseeing all the processes in the organization as well as managing relationships with outside groups.

When it comes to making critical decisions, executive directors find themselves in the middle in a couple of significant ways. First, they have to balance the interests of the organization with those of outside parties, such as community groups and funders. Second, they have to balance the strategic interests of the board with the operational interests of the staff. In both cases, they have the primary role of communicating the details of the decision so that there is sufficient buy-in from all the parties.

Any critical decision that significantly changes the programming or operations of an organization and the allocation of existing and future resources is a decision where the executive director has to take a lead role. It is the executive's role to keep the organization whole—that is, to keep the programming and operations aligned with the nonprofits' mission and to keep the organization within its budget.

Next, we set out two examples of situations where executive directors should be the primary decision makers. As with the previous examples, we are sure most of our readers have faced similar situations themselves or know an executive who has.

A Funder Initiative

In the course of their work, many funders—including foundations, government agencies, corporations, and individual donors—actively look for ways that their grantees can better meet community needs and meet them more efficiently. Based on their own research, donors set up pools of money to initiate new programs and improvements in nonprofit capacity. In these situations, funders issue requests for proposals or approach specific nonprofits to take part in the initiative.

If the initiative clearly falls within the scope of the nonprofit's plans, there is really no choice to be made: everyone sees the potential benefits of taking part in the initiative. However, if there are points of disagreement, the situation can become politically sensitive. Executive directors are in the position to evaluate the potential impact of the initiative on staff and operations, discuss any strategy or policy issues with the board, and work with the funder to determine fit and negotiate on behalf of the organization. When the organization cannot take on the initiative and must turn it down, the executive director's tact and communication skills are key to maintaining good funder relations for the future.

An Unexpected Financial Shortfall

At times organizations face a significant unanticipated loss of income. Earned income can be affected by decreases in the number of clients served. Arts organizations know that poor weather can have a dramatic impact on attendance. And many human service organizations have experienced the effects of increased competition with both other nonprofit and for-profit providers. Similarly, sudden changes in donor priorities or financial position can affect anticipated gifts. Promised gifts can be withdrawn, donors can change the timetable for payments, or in the case of stock, the actual value of the gift can change significantly.

In these situations, executive directors are faced with major budget variances and have to make midcourse corrections to prevent a large deficit at the end of the year. This requires working with the staff leadership to determine how the shortfall can be managed with minimum short- and long-term damage to the organization and community. In most cases, the executive will be facing a cutback decision, which might mean eliminating staff, closing a facility, or reducing services.

Using the Matrix

In both of these situations, the executive director plays the primary decision-making role. He or she has to incorporate the information and opinions of a range of groups—internal and external—that will be affected by the outcome. The matrix can help collect and organize this detailed information, which will provide the executive a comprehensive overview of the situation and make the appropriate trade-offs. The matrix can also be used to communicate the points of view of the groups involved in the process and help the executive build consensus for the decision as the process unfolds.

Managers

Obviously something slipped through here.

—Reverend John Vaughan, financial administrator for the Archdiocese of Miami (when asked why it held stock in companies that manufacture contraceptives)

Whether they deal with programmatic activities or administration, nonprofit managers are on the front lines of the organization and make it work on a daily basis. Unlike the executive directors, who take a broad view of the organization, managers tend to focus on their particular department or area of expertise, so they tend to rely on their own specialized professional expertise and that of the group they oversee.

In making most routine decisions, the manager's depth of experience and knowledge work to the organization's advantage. However, it can be problematic when managers make critical decisions.

Groups within organizations can become "siloed." That is, they become so focused on the particulars of their own jobs and work group that they become isolated from the rest of the organization. Problems arise when they filter out new and important information because they are so locked into their own routine. Significant information can be omitted or slip through. In making critical decisions, managers need a way to break out of their silo—their usual way of doing things—and incorporate a wider range of information. They have to determine not only how the decision will affect their own team, but how it will affect the rest of the organization and the community it serves.

Here are two common examples that illustrate how managers often approach critical decisions and the negative consequences this can have for the organization. Again, many of our readers have dealt with the fallout from similar decisions when they are made and implemented in a management silo.

Adding a New Project or Program

Most nonprofit professionals are driven by the desire to meet community needs. As a result, staff are continually developing new programming ideas or better ways to deliver existing programs or services. In addition, they are usually active within their own professional communities and make efforts to learn about innovative programs and best practices from their colleagues.

Ideas for new projects and programs often emerge from staff outside the normal planning and budgeting cycle. Someone goes to a conference or talks with a community leader, and the idea is born. If the idea has worked in a similar organization or there seems to be a pressing community need, the staff might embrace it, and a process of emotional decision making is set in motion.

In many cases, new activities are implemented without a thorough review. As a result, they can strain the resource base of the department or organization, set one group at odds with another, or have considerably less than the anticipated impact in the community.

Managers, along with their staff, can also become too invested in the activity to give it a thorough review to see whether it is indeed feasible or practical. They need a way to maintain emotional distance and collect the appropriate range of information to evaluate the decision.

Adding New Technology

As hardware and software become less expensive, many purchasing decisions are made at the department or work group level. If the nonprofit has no comprehensive technology plan or computer specialist on staff, this is more likely to happen. If technology decisions are made in isolation, they can actually decrease productivity.

A careful decision requires that the manager determine how the new technology will affect specific jobs, the resources required for training and support as well as for the initial purchase, and how it will be integrated with other technology and systems in the organization. Neglecting any one of these areas can result in acquiring technology that might not be used, or might not be used to its fullest potential. It might also result in a system that is redundant, cumbersome, and inefficient.

A manager must collect information about a proposed technology, how it will be used, and what it will take to implement and integrate it with existing systems. This requires going outside the work group to other parts of the organization. It is also likely to require consulting with a specialist who has the appropriate technical expertise.

Using the Matrix

The matrix can be especially useful for managers working in nonprofits because it provides them with a structure for moving beyond their silos. Instead of reacting to new opportunities, they carefully assess and stage any innovative ideas with the due diligence process. The matrix can also be used as a learning tool for staff as the manager goes through the process. It requires them to acknowledge and then address larger issues related to the choice: strategic alignment, budget, and expertise. This will move them beyond their immediate jobs and departments to a broader organizational perspective.

Funders

> *Philanthropy is the refuge of rich people who*
> *wish to annoy their fellow creatures.*
>
> *—Oscar Wilde*

Funding organizations—government agencies, corporate sponsorship and charitable giving programs, and private foundations—are all faced with the challenge of allocating their limited resources in ways that are most efficient and effective. In addition, they are compelled to do this in ways that are fair and easily communicated to nonprofits seeking funds, as well as to the public. In recent years, there has been a greater emphasis on the assessment and evaluation of giving programs, as well as viewing philanthropy as an investment activity. Some have adopted a venture philanthropy approach based on commercial investment practices. For these reasons, the due diligence process and matrix tool can be highly useful in supporting charitable giving. This approach can be used by grant makers to make the best use of their limited staff time and financial resources. Here is how.

Providing a Consistent Review Process

Philanthropic professionals sometimes review grant proposals themselves and sometimes enlist review panels with specialized expertise. In many cases, they already use guiding questions and sometimes assessment grids. However, these questions and grids are often based on the immediate substantive merit of the proposal and may not address issues of risk or sustainability in sufficient detail. The decision criteria might not be weighted, or the scoring might not be sufficiently scaled to accommodate a range of reviewer opinions. The due diligence process and the matrix can be used to enrich the tools and processes grant makers currently have in place.

Evening the Playing Field

There's a rule: the more general the grant criteria, the greater the variety in applications. For example, funds that are set up to support new program development, general operating support, or management capacity building will attract a wide range of projects from a wide range of organizations. The matrix provides a way to compare different proposals with criteria that go beyond the specific content and address risk, leverage—philanthropic return—and sustainability.

Drawing Sharp Distinctions

Some grant pools fund very similar projects, such as specific staff training or the purchase of computer hardware. In these cases, grant makers are faced with drawing distinctions between applicants based on details in the proposal. The matrix provides a way to weight the differences so that the choices can be made on even minor but meaningful differences.

Giving Feedback to Applicants

The matrix can help in communicating and discussing the grant decision. When a proposal has been successful, summary information can underscore its strengths. And when a proposal is denied, funders can use the matrix data to explain the comparative weaknesses of the proposal and thereby promote learning and dialogue. This should be viewed as constructive and position the applicants to make stronger, more competitive proposals next time. For example, applicants might benefit from developing a more detailed budget or better describing how the proposed activity supports the organization's overall strategy.

The due diligence process lays out a standard and relatively simple review process for funders. The matrix can help individual philanthropists as well as review panels assess proposal content in a consistent way. Finally, it provides a means for communicating the decisions of the grant makers in detail.

Consultants

My greatest strength as a consultant is to be
ignorant and ask a few questions.

—*Peter Drucker*

Consultants come in many forms: facilitators, technicians, strategists, evaluators, mentors, analysts, financial advisers, and program experts, among many others. There are lots of consultants who do a wide variety of things in the nonprofit world, but they have one thing in common: they consult. That is, they offer advice; they do not make decisions. If consultants cross the line and start making decisions, they have by definition moved into a management role. Unless a consultant has specifically been hired to temporarily fill a staff function, this can lead to considerable ambiguity and problems.

The consultant's proper job is to help leadership, board, executive director, or managers make decisions—often critical decisions. Of course, managers are usually comfortable making routine decisions without outside help. Sometimes consultants carry out research or provide information based on their experience in the field. These consultants are referred to as content experts. At other times, they guide the decision-making process. These are referred to as process consultants. Some consultants do both. Whichever role a consultant uses, the due diligence process and matrix tool can be extremely helpful to them in several ways.

Guiding the Decision Process

Consultants are in a position to instruct their clients in the use of the due diligence process. Whether they are deciding to purchase a new building, develop a new program area, or retrench part of their operation, the process can guide the group's work. When the engagement is over, the consultant leaves the client with a deliverable: the resulting decision and a new set of skills.

Presenting Data

When consultants provide expert information to support a decision, they can use the matrix tool to present it. They can also include their own opinions about the criteria. For instance, if a consultant is asked to assess the feasibility of a new program, each of the due diligence criteria can serve as headings to organize a detailed advisory report. Findings in each category can then be presented clearly. If an organization is considering several options for retrenchment, the consultant can compare benefits and trade-offs in a similar way.

Preparing Consulting Reports

Whether a consultant uses due diligence and the matrix to facilitate the process or frame expert advice, both will capture a great deal of information in an organized way over the course of the project. At the end of most consulting engagements, the consultant provides a report detailing the work done and the results achieved. The process and matrix tool provide a means of recording the work and the results as they progress, and they make documentation richer and easier. In other words, the consulting report is essentially written by the end of the project.

The method provides consultants with a practical tool to use in the complex situations they often face. This approach can complement the process or the content expertise they bring to their engagements. And it can provide a way of summarizing their work to improve their reports and deliverables.

———————————

How due diligence and the matrix are used in nonprofits depends on who is using them. And as we've seen in this chapter, this approach not only supports critical decisions at various levels within the organization, but can also enrich a nonprofit's working relationship with funders and consultants. It's a practical and robust approach with multiple applications. The next and final chapter provides a checklist to help guide you through the process.

10

The Decision-Making Guide

*We must give lengthy deliberation to what
has to be decided once and for all.*

—Publilius Syrus (c. 100 B.C.)

WE END THIS BOOK by providing a summary guide to help you
work through critical decisions as they arise. We said at the beginning that our goal was to be practical, and so we end on a practical note.

The next time a staff, board, or community member comes to you with
what he or she sees as an exciting opportunity or major challenge, use the following series of questions. First, use it to assess the importance and complexity
of the decision. Then, if you are facing a complex and critical decision, use it
to help guide you and your organization through the due diligence process.

Assessing the Decision

For the following questions, select the response that applies to your situation:

1. What kind of decision is this?

   a. Habitual (routine, informal, we do it all the time without thinking)

   b. Recipe (we have an established process for dealing with this)

   c. Planning (we will address it as part of our routine strategic or
      operational planning processes)

   d. None of the above

If you select a, b, or c, you are not dealing with a critical decision and don't have to go any further because you can rely on one of your established processes. If you answer d, you should confirm that you are dealing with a critical decision by moving to question 2.

2. Does the decision have any of the following characteristics?

    a. We've never dealt with a situation like this before. (It's novel.)

    b. It will have a major impact on the organization either positive or negative. (It's risky.)

    c. We feel that we have to make the decision and take action as soon as possible. (There's an urge to react rather than respond.)

If you select any of the three choices, you are facing a critical decision, and the due diligence approach would be helpful. Go on to question 3, and begin organizing the process. Otherwise go back to question 1, and figure out exactly what you missed.

3. Whose decision is it?

    a. Who are the primary decision makers? (those with the authority to make the decision and ultimately held responsible for its outcome)

    b. Who should inform the decision? (those with specialized expert or practical knowledge that would support the process)

    c. Who should be informed of the decision? (those with a role in the successful implementation of the decision)

Make a list identifying specific individuals and groups in each category. Once the decision-making roles are clarified, you are ready to start addressing the decision itself in question 4.

4. What kind of decision is this?

    a. Feasibility (we want to see if something is possible).

    b. Pilot (we want to try something out on a limited basis).

    c. Implementation (we want to fully put into place something that has already been tested).

    d. Cutback (we want to reduce or eliminate something).

If you see that the decision neatly falls into one of these categories (stages), you can go to the appropriate matrix. However, if what is being proposed cuts across more than one category, break the decision down into stages, and start with the earliest stage. For example, if what is being proposed is to assess the feasibility and also test something, start with the feasibility portion of the decision, and postpone the second part of the decision, the test, until you have the results from the first stage. Go to question 5 to weight the matrix.

5. How do we weight the matrix?

   a. Who should be involved in assigning weights? (This is the person who best understands the risk, leverage, and sustainability issues associated with the decision.)

   b. What weights should be assigned to each of the decision criteria? (Distribute 100 weighting points among the criteria based on importance.)

Once you identify who is most appropriate for assigning weights to the matrix criteria and they assign them, you are ready to move on to clarifying the types of options you'll evaluate. Go to question 6.

6. What are our options?

   a. Binary (either we do it or we don't).

   b. Similar (we are choosing between options that for the most part are the same but differ in some ways).

   c. Dissimilar (we are choosing among very different options).

After you identify which of the three categories of options you will be working with, you can complete your matrix by incorporating the weighted criteria and range of options. You will now have a grid ready for scoring, so move on to the next stage.

Working Through the Matrix

Use the following guide as a checklist for working through the matrix:

1. How to score the matrix:

   ☑ Use a process that first allows individual scoring of the matrix to collect the widest range of opinions.

☑ Then compare the data to show points of agreement and disagreement.

☑ Finally, engage in discussion and constructive feedback about the results to allow decision makers to incorporate new information and refine their final scores.

Once you have developed a scoring and recording process that incorporates all three elements, you are ready to score the options. After the scores have been added up, move on to the next item.

2. How to evaluate the scores:

☑ Determine how much risk is associated with each option. The scores represent the level of success or failure anticipated if you choose an option.

☑ Determine whether the risk is reasonable. Does the anticipated benefit to the organization justify the risk?

If you determine that the risk is too great, do not implement the decision. If the risk is appropriate, implement the decision. Then move on to the next item.

3. How to inform the appropriate stakeholders of the decision:

☑ Go back to the individuals and groups identified in item 3 in "Assessing the Decision" as "should be informed." These are stakeholders who in some cases will be affected by the decision if it is implemented and in others if it is not.

☑ Inform them of the decision according to the plans developed for communicating the process and decision, using the results of the matrix analysis where appropriate.

☑ Resolve any issues related to the decision. You are ready to monitor the impact of the decision with help from the matrix. Go on to the next item.

4. How to evaluate the impact of the decision:

☑ Develop periodic review and reporting processes based on the due diligence criteria. For example, is the decision having the anticipated measurable impact? Are we on budget? Have we built the intended relationships with collaborating organizations?

☑ Develop processes for overall evaluation of the decision. How do we know whether we have succeeded or failed?

Once you have evaluated the impact of the decision and determined whether it has worked or hasn't, you will understand why. You are then ready to move to the next stage of the process if appropriate or learn in a structured way from this decision.

Staff Renewal Decisions

THIS BOOK HAS DEALT with a progression of decisions, each representing a stage in the life cycle of an idea. Chapters Five through Eight each treated a stage in the due diligence process: feasibility, pilot, implementation, and cutback. There is another type of choice that is important to any organization's development and can be made at any stage in its evolution. We call these renewal decisions, and they are tied to a key resource in any nonprofit: its people.

While structures, programs, and processes can become obsolete, human resources are renewable. Staff and volunteers can develop and even be transformed by expanding their knowledge and acquiring new skills. As they learn and grow intellectually, they become a more valuable asset to the organization. Because they play a pivotal role in providing service to the community, decisions tied to staff development can have a major effect on organizational performance.

Anyone working in the sector understands the pivotal role that human resources play in the development and delivery of programming and services. They also understand the challenges of maintaining a current staff and volunteer force. Funders have recently taken a new interest in management capacity and staff development and have begun to support a range of staff training and development efforts. This appendix first provides an overview of these human resource issues. Then it shows how the matrix can be used in a slightly modified format to review staff development decisions. To be consistent with the rest of the book, we conclude with a brief illustrative minicase.

The Human Element in Service Organizations

For the past quarter-century, the United States has truly been a service economy, that is, an economy based on the provision of services rather than the production of goods. The majority of American jobs are service jobs, where the actual work or labor done for someone else is the product. While this is new to the commercial sector, which has seen a growing number of service jobs, government and nonprofits have always been devoted to the provision of services.

Service workers fall into one of two categories: unskilled or highly skilled. Unskilled service workers are usually associated with minimum wage employment in commercial enterprises such as fast-food restaurants. Highly skilled service workers are employed in positions across all sectors and make up the professional and managerial workforce. These individuals are also referred to as knowledge workers because their qualifications are based on mastery of specialized knowledge.

The majority of the nonprofit workforce consists of individuals with the specific training and, in many cases, the credentials and licenses, required for their jobs. Social workers, doctors, lawyers, educators, and accountants are examples. The quality of the organization's programming and services is dependent on the knowledge these individuals bring to the organization. And developing and sustaining that knowledge base is key to the viability of individual organizations and the sector.

Nonprofits are dependent on the quality of the information their staff and, in some cases, volunteers possess. Basic education and training provide the base on which to build staff expertise. For example, skills such as critical thinking and the ability to analyze quantitative data are critical to program professionals and managers. They are fundamental skills that allow staff members to understand and learn more about the world as they progress in their jobs and careers.

However, basic skills are not enough in a world and nonprofit sector that is becoming increasingly specialized and fast paced. Nonprofit professionals must constantly be upgrading their skills to keep them current with the requirements of their jobs. In the dynamic nonprofit environment, developing expertise to meet the range of challenges an organization might face is essential.

Because change is often driven by technology based in both the hard and social sciences, knowledge workers are constantly upgrading their technical skills. Individuals need the ability to use new information systems and databases, master new leadership tools, and become proficient in the latest professional competencies. The more a person knows about his or her work and organization, the more valuable that person becomes. This person is then able to deliver a better quality of service and do it more efficiently. Also, the more individuals know, the further they can progress in their careers, in either a specific job or series of jobs or in making an impact in their fields.

Training and education become the vehicle for organizational adaptation during challenging times. By learning what is relevant for the communities they serve and how to deliver it, nonprofit knowledge workers enable their organizations to maintain strategic focus and provide services of value.

Organizational Capacity and Staff Development

In the manufacturing sector, a business's capacity (that is, how much product it can make) is tied to its plant and equipment. A nonprofit's organizational capacity, or its ability to serve the community, is in large measure dependent on the skills and expertise of its staff. If a nonprofit is to maintain capacity, it must continuously update staff knowledge so that staff members will at least stay current in their field. If the nonprofit is to increase capacity, it will have to enhance that knowledge base, so that the staff becomes capable of working smarter.

Training and educational programs are a primary vehicle for building capacity in nonprofits. Policymakers and foundation representatives increasingly view investment in these activities as critical to developing a viable sector in the current environment. A number of national and intermediary organizations have increasingly expanded their role of providing training and coaching. Renewing staff by providing them with the opportunities to expand their knowledge is viewed as necessary for organizational and sector stability.

The costs associated with staff compensation are usually the largest item in most nonprofit organizations' operating budgets. Across the sector, costs tied to salary and benefits have been increasing significantly in recent years. In contrast, most nonprofits have a very small line for staff development and training, and many smaller organizations have none at all and support education only through discretionary funds. There is often no specific policy that guides the allocation of limited training dollars; opportunities or requests are handled on a case-by-case basis.

Given the importance of staff renewal and the limited resources available, a due diligence process is helpful in supporting decisions that align training opportunities with organizational needs. The process outlined in this appendix is based on criteria developed for assessing any innovation and therefore can be used for any change where risk, leverage, and sustainability have to be considered to some extent. We can use some of the due diligence criteria to assess how to put new knowledge to work in the organization most appropriately. Similar matrices and approaches can be developed for other resource renewal issues such as renegotiating a lease, buying or purchasing equipment, or changing the mix of programming or services offered. In each of these cases, criteria important and specific to each organization would be selected, and a matrix constructed similar to the one presented next.

The Staff Renewal Matrix

The staff renewal matrix in Exhibit A.1 has fewer criteria than the decision matrices in previous chapters. There are two reasons for this. First, staff renewal decisions are limited in scope; they usually involve individuals or a small group and address a specific area of activity. Second, the risk or downside of inappropriate training is minimal; the worst that can happen is that staff members learn something irrelevant to their work. The weighted criteria include focus on issues of organization fit, that is, how the training program supports existing programs and relationships. As with the other

Exhibit A.1. Sample Staff Renewal Matrix.			
Criteria	Weight	Decision Maker Score	Weighted Score
Strategic alignment	20		
Expertise	18		
Reasonable cost	17		
Measurable impact	15		
Measurable productivity	10		
Organization development	10		
Broader benefit	5		
Risk factors	3		
Board oversight	2		
Totals	100	0	0
Total possible weighted score			1,000
Percentage agreement			%

matrices, the more heavily weighted a factor is, the more important it is to minimizing risk, maximizing leverage, and ensuring sustainability of the outcome.

Staff Renewal Criteria

A set of questions for each of the criteria that guide the decision maker in scoring follows. As with the previous matrices, if the decision maker can answer each precisely with the specific information required, a higher score will result. If the decision maker cannot answer the questions or the answers do not support the decision criteria, the score will be lower.

Strategic Alignment

Strategic alignment is the most heavily weighted of the criteria. Staff development should support an organization's current strategy: its plans for the future reflected in its values, vision, mission, program and organizational goals, and allocation of resources. The most valuable staff development efforts support and advance the organization's highest-priority action items outlined in its strategic plan in significant ways.

Questions to Ask to Assess Strategic Alignment

☑ How, specifically, does proposed staff renewal support the organization's current role in the community, reflected in its mission, goals, and values?

☑ How does this staff renewal effort fit within the organization's existing strategic and operating plans? Which specific goals and activities does it support? How does it do so?

☑ What is the potential strategic impact of the staff renewal effort? That is, does it significantly contribute to the organization's ability to pursue major high-priority action items that will have a large effect on the organization overall? Or will it only marginally contribute to minor, low-priority items that affect only specific programs or departments?

Once the decision makers understand in detail how the proposed staff development will complement the organization's plans, they assign a score. The better the fit and the greater the potential positive impact on advancing the strategy are, the higher the score will be.

Expertise

Developing the staff's knowledge and skill base depends on external expertise. The sources of information, educational programming, or coaching can vary greatly. It is important to review and assess them to determine how well they will meet the needs of specific staff.

Questions to Ask to Assess Expertise

☑ What type of expertise is best suited to supporting staff development? A detailed inventory of the knowledge or skills needed should be developed, along with an assessment of the most appropriate method for assessing those skills.

☑ Is there expertise within the organization? That is, has someone on staff demonstrated expertise in the appropriate area, and is this person able to impart what he or she knows to others? Sometimes staff renewal can be an internal process.

☑ If the expertise must be obtained from outside the organization, where will it come from? Decision makers must identify the most appropriate source. Issues such as quality and accessibility should be addressed.

☑ If the expertise is obtained from outside the organization, how is transfer of knowledge assured? The decision makers should assess what is realistically requiring to develop and train staff, along with the cost.

The greater the availability of appropriate expertise and transferability of the resulting knowledge are, the higher the decision makers' score will be.

Reasonable Cost

Understanding how much the staff development will cost to implement and sustain is critical. Costs can vary widely, from modest costs for one-time training sessions that are clearly defined to significant costs for continuing education requiring credentialing. A comprehensive analysis of the full range of costs and budget projections should accompany any proposal for staff renewal.

Questions to Ask to Assess Cost

☑ What are all the costs associated with initiating and sustaining this proposed staff renewal effort? A budget should be developed that contains direct and indirect costs, fixed and variable costs, and sunk versus relevant future costs. A clearly detailed narrative should accompany the budget detailing the reasoning supporting each line.

☑ Are the amounts budgeted realistic? The decision makers should review the assumptions made about the amounts required in each budget line.

☑ Where will the resources in the budget come from? Each line item should be tied to a reliable source of funds.

The greater the decision makers' confidence is in the accuracy of the budget, the higher their scores will be.

Measurable Impact

It is critical to be able to assess whether the staff renewal effort is effective and to what degree. That is, there has to be a way of knowing if the training works and to what extent. Setting clear and measurable goals, such as passing a certification exam or mastering a method, is the first step in assessing impact. It forms the basis for monitoring the impact of new knowledge on the organization. Being able to determine the organizational change, either positive or negative, is also critical for objectively determining if the effort is successful.

Questions to Ask to Assess Impact

☑ What is the intended impact of the staff renewal effort? The level of impact should also be set as a specific goal or target that management believes is realistic and achievable.

☑ How will that impact be measured? The indicators should be established and provision for monitoring developed. A target number within a specific time frame should be established as a baseline for success. In addition, the monitoring process should be consistent with any existing review and evaluation processes.

The more clearly defined and measurable the impact is, the higher the decision makers' scores will be.

Measurable Productivity

Ideally, new knowledge should result in increased efficiencies in addition to the desired impact or effectiveness. It should enable the staff to work smarter and better leverage the nonprofit's limited resources.

Once again, productivity can be measured by dividing the results obtained by the resources expended. For example, if training in report software allows staff to reduce the amount of time spent on routine paperwork, there is a measurable increase in productivity. In this case, the time spent before and after training would be compared to determine precisely how much is gained.

Question to Ask to Assess Productivity

☑ If the proposed staff development effort is successful, will it have a measurable impact on the organization's productivity? If so, the positive or negative impact should be defined in a measurable way.

The greater the anticipated productivity and the more accurate and reliable the measures are, the higher the decision makers' scores will be.

Organization Development

Expanding the knowledge base of the nonprofit can position the organization to do more and better work in the future.

Question to Ask to Assess Organization Development

☑ How will the proposed staff renewal contribute to the development of the organization in the following areas: staff (both personally and professionally), programming, and administration? Clearly, any effort should increase the staff's skill sets and work toward meeting their personal and professional goals. If the effort is at odds with their goals, there will be a significant problem. If the effort is tied to programming, it should enhance the organization's existing and planned activities by increasing content, quality, or reach. Finally, if it is administrative, it should have the potential for making the organization's work processes more efficient and effective.

The more that staff renewal will contribute to staff, program, and administrative development, the higher the decision makers' scores will be.

Broader Benefit

If knowledge is successfully transferred to an organization, it might be viable and productive in other organizational settings. The innovation can be diffused to a broader group, internally or externally.

Questions to Ask to Assess Broader Benefit

☑ If the staff development effort is successfully implemented, are there benefits that extend beyond the individuals directly involved? The benefits should be articulated in detail, and the individuals and groups that would profit should be identified.

☑ How will the knowledge be further disseminated? Detailed plans for circulating information should be developed.

The greater the number of individuals, groups, and organizations identified that might benefit and the more specific the dissemination plans are, the higher the decision makers' scores will be.

Risk Factors

The decision makers should speculate about what could go wrong as a result of the staff development effort to assess how well equipped the organization is to correct any potential problems. This factor is not weighted as heavily as it is in other decision contexts because the risk is largely contained in the personnel area.

Personnel risk can take one of two forms. First, if the staff renewal effort is not successful and the individuals do not acquire the knowledge as planned, there will be no benefit to the organization, and resources will have been wasted. Second, there can be some significant risks if the effort is successful. The added skills or credentials might position the staff members for other jobs in the local labor market. There is always the risk that through education efforts for staff, the organization is preparing staff members for their next employer.

Questions to Assess Risk

☑ What are the potential consequences of unsuccessful staff renewal? The decision makers should entertain a range of what-if scenarios in each area and determine the most likely organizational response. If there are adequate safeguards in place, the risks can be managed.

☑ Are there any potential negative consequences, especially in terms of staff retention, if the effort is successful? The decision makers should develop a set of contingencies if these negative consequences result.

The fewer the potential risks there are and the better the organization is able to manage them if they do occur, the higher the decision makers' scores will be.

Board Oversight

Board oversight processes should address staff renewal in a structured way. Because these are usually personnel decisions carried out without direct board involvement, one of the most appropriate ways is through human resource policies that set guidelines for staff renewal.

Question to Ask to Assess Board Oversight

☑ Does the board have the appropriate structures, processes, and policies in place to oversee staff development? The way in which reporting about the decision is reflected in board policies and ongoing committee work should provide the answers.

The more closely matched these staff renewal efforts are with existing board oversight mechanisms, the higher the decision makers' scores will be.

In reviewing the criteria and completing the matrix, the decision makers learn more about proposed activities and the potential impact on staff and the organization. They will have collected and organized sufficient information to support their decision and communicate it to the appropriate individuals and groups, internally and externally. The minicase that follows shows how the matrix can be used in assessing a staff renewal effort.

THE CASE OF THE NEIGHBORHOOD IMPROVEMENT CORPORATION

The Neighborhood Improvement Corporation is a medium-sized urban nonprofit that works with low-income home owners to repair and upgrade private residences and improve public spaces. The organization has been successful and is relatively stable, with the exception of some recent staff turnover in three key senior positions: the chief financial officer (CFO), the director of operations, and the director of programming. All were the result of normal attrition: one was a retirement and the two others the result of moves to other cities. The executive director, Ms. Miller, was able to hire qualified but relatively inexperienced staff for each position. Ms. Ray is the new CFO, Mr. White is the director of operations, and Mr. Blaine is the program director.

The corporation now faces undertaking a new strategic planning process. Ms. Miller has extensive experience with planning and strategy, but her new staff do not. She has already decided that it would be a good use of the organization's limited training funds to put the staff members through the same course in strategic planning. She is also planning to take the course herself, both as a refresher and to build a cohesive senior management group.

Ms. Miller finds two university-based programs that provide an overview of strategic planning for nonprofit professionals. The first is housed at a major research university and is part of its larger set of degree and continuing education offerings for nonprofit managers. It is a short course, with the class meeting for three hours once a week over eight weeks. The second is housed at a smaller university with a greater emphasis on the local community. This school has a nonprofit center that provides an array of workshops and consulting services for local nonprofits. Its strategic planning program is a one-day workshop that meets on a weekday.

Ms. Miller is familiar with the due diligence process and using the matrix. She assigns weights to the staff renewal criteria and uses the tool to compare the two alternatives. A summary of how she views and scores each option is described below.

Option 1: The Eight-Week Short Course

Strategic alignment. The program addresses the strategic planning and implementation and will be used to support the corporation's next strategy process. Score: 10.

Expertise. The instructor has a doctorate in management strategy and policy and is the director of the university's nonprofit executive programs. She has written several books on the subject, has extensive expertise, and has been working as a consultant to non-profits on issues of strategy and implementation nationally. Score: 10.

Reasonable cost. The cost of the course would be $1,000 per person, or $4,000 total. Because the course is held after work hours, there would be no costs for staff replacements or any associated with lost productivity. Ms. Miller realizes that this university has the highest prices in the area for executive training. However, after some additional research, she also realizes that its offerings are comparable to similar courses offered at major institutions nationally. Score: 9.

Measurable impact. The course description states that the approach to the material is based on organizational self-study and application of planning techniques to one's own organization. At the end of the course, students will have developed a planning process that is appropriate for their own organizations and have carried out part of the analysis that should go into the process. The corporation staff will have learned not only about planning conceptually but actually started to work on its own plan. Score: 10.

Measurable productivity. It is assumed that if the staff jointly develops the strategy process, they will be able to engage the board and the relevant stakeholders more efficiently. However, the emphasis of this effort is on developing effective, not efficient planners, so productivity improvements are not necessarily expected, and no measurements have been developed. Score: 3.

Organization development. The course should help to build a coherent management team that has an overview of all the phases of planning, including implementation and monitoring. This will position the staff for further development in the areas of program and project planning and assessment and evaluation. Score: 8.

Broader benefit. The management team members will be able to transfer what they learn to the board and staff. This will ensure that the knowledge base related to planning is diffused through the organization. There are no plans to disseminate what is learned externally. Score: 7.

Risk factors. The only risk that Ms. Miller sees is that the training and additional skills would support Ms. Ray's, Mr. White's, and Mr. Blaine's next career move. However, since they have all been recently hired, she feels that this is not likely to occur soon. Score: 8.

Board oversight. The corporation has limited personnel policies that cover staff training and development. They simply state that training must be directly applicable to staff members' job requirements and that corporation funds cannot be used for credit-bearing degree programs. The course meets the policy guidelines. Score: 10.

Option 2: The One-Day Workshop

Strategic alignment. The workshop addresses the strategic planning but does not address implementation, so it will support only a portion of the corporation's upcoming planning activities. Score: 7.

Expertise. This university's workshops are based on a peer education model. A local nonprofit executive director will lead the discussion. He heads a small arts organization, and his experience has been exclusively in the cultural arena. It is not clear to Ms. Miller how much of his experience will be applicable to an organization like the corporation. Score: 4.

Reasonable cost. This university has played a major role in the local nonprofit community for the past twenty years. Its education programming is viewed by several local foundations as critical to developing local management capacity. As a result, it heavily subsidizes the workshops. The cost of the workshop for each participant is $75, for a total of $300. There will be minimal lost productivity because the workshop is held in a single session on a weekday. Score: 10.

Measurable impact. The staff will receive an overview of how to formulate a strategy. They will not receive detailed information or have the opportunity to work on their own planning process because of the time limitations of the workshop format. Score: 4.

Measurable productivity. Ms. Miller sees no direct effect on productivity. Score: 0.

Organization development. The workshop will provide the staff with a common understanding of what part of the planning process involves. This would position them to go on to learn more. Score: 3.

Broader benefit. The approach learned might be used to help structure the corporation's strategy process. Score: 2.

Risk factors. There is a risk that the workshop will not provide enough information for the group because it addresses only a portion of the planning process or that the instructor's experience might not be relevant for the corporation. Score: 5.

Board oversight. The workshop meets the policy guidelines set by the corporation's board. The training is consistent with what is required in their jobs and is not part of a credit-bearing course of study. Score: 10.

Ms. Miller compares the scores and decides that the eight-week short course is the appropriate choice. The short course scored 87 percent agreement and the workshop 52 percent.

She is able to justify allocating a large part of the corporation's annual training budget to the activity based on its overall value to the staff and organization. Ms. Miller's scores are summarized in Exhibit A.2.

Criteria	Weight	Option 1: Eight-Week Course	Option 1 Weighted Score	Option 2: One-Day Workshop	Option 2 Weighted Score
Strategic alignment	20	10	200	7	140
Expertise	18	10	180	4	72
Reasonable cost	17	9	153	10	170
Measurable impact	15	10	150	4	60
Measurable productivity	10	3	30	0	0
Organization development	10	8	80	3	30
Broader benefit	5	7	35	2	10
Risk factors	3	8	24	5	15
Board oversight	2	10	20	10	20
Totals	**100**	**75**	**872**	**45**	**517**
Total possible weighted score			**1,000**		**1,000**
Percentage agreement			**87%**		**52%**

Exhibit A.2. Summary of Ms. Miller's Scores.

NOTES

Chapter One

1. For a comprehensive and accessible overview of decision-making concepts and methods, see J. G. March, *A Primer on Decision Making: How Decisions Happen* (New York: Free Press, 1994).

2. *Heuristic* means a replicable approach to learning, discovery or problem solving, introduced in the fourth century by the mathematician Pappus of Alexandria. Heuristics, the study of these replicable methods, has influenced a number of fields, including philosophy, law, and computer science. Studies of the psychological dimensions of heuristics in decision making resulted from the seminal work of A. Tversky and D. Kahneman in *Judgment Under Uncertainty: Heuristics and Biases*, Daniel Kahneman, Amos Tversky and Paul Slovic (eds.) (Cambridge: Cambridge University Press, 1982). Later work by G. Gigerenzer and P. Todd and their colleagues at the ABC research group demonstrates how heuristics can be used to make

effective decisions quickly and efficiently. Their work is presented in *Simple Heuristics That Make Us Smart* (New York: Oxford University Press, 1999).

3. The best introduction, in our opinion, to why and how bureaucracies are formed and behave can be found in the classic writings of the nineteenth-century social theorist Max Weber. This work can be found in H. H. Gerth and C. Wright Mills (eds.), *From Max Weber: Essays in Sociology* (New York: Oxford University Press, 1946).

4. Our use of the term *recipe decision* is rooted in the philosopher of social science Alfred Schutz's concept of recipe knowledge: the practical knowledge of how to do something, without necessarily understanding why the process works, in a given type of situation. Recipe knowledge leads to scripted decisions. By extension, scripted decisions are recipe decisions. For an explication of recipe knowledge and how it leads to recipe decision making, consult A. Shutz and T. Luckmann, *The Structure of the Life World* (Portsmouth, N.H.: Heinemann, 1972), and the subsequent work of P. Berger and T. Luckmann that builds on Schutz's ideas, *The Social Construction of Reality: A Treatise in the Sociology of Knowledge* (New York: Penguin, 1976).

5. For example, the U.S. Small Business Association supports the Web site www.business.gov, which provides links to the recipes for complying with government regulations. The Nonprofit Financial Center (www.nfconline.org/main/info/library) offers a library of reference books that provide standard recipes to guide organizations through reporting and tax compliance processes.

6. A *standard* is a level of quality that is accepted as a norm for a certain group of organizations. Nonprofits as a whole have a number of sector-wide standards that are used in support of decision making. For example, the Better Business Bureau's Wise Giving Alliance has developed a set of standards to guide nonprofits in their fundraising (www.give.or/standards/index.asp). And the Maryland

Association of Nonprofit Organizations has put into place an accreditation process based on an ethics and accountability code that sets standards for management and governance (www. marylandnonprofits.org/html/standards).

7. The concept of *best practice,* which has gained considerable currency in the past decade, actually was central to models of efficient and effective management early in the twentieth century. Frederick Winslow Taylor introduced the notion of *one best method* in his classic work, *The Principles of Scientific Management* (New York: HarperCollins, 1919).

8. See P. R. Niven, *Balanced Scorecard Step-by-Step for Government and Nonprofit Agencies* (Hoboken, N.J.: Wiley, 2003).

9. See M. R. Edwards and A. J. Ewen, *360 Degree Feedback: The Powerful New Model for Employee Assessment and Performance Improvement* (New York: AMACOM, 1996).

10. For an overview of nonprofit planning processes, see J. M. Bryson, *Strategic Planning for Public and Nonprofit Organizations: A Guide to Strengthening and Sustaining Organizational Achievement,* 3rd ed. (San Francisco: Jossey-Bass, 2004).

11. For a recent overview of the conditions contributing to the complex issues facing nonprofits, see L. M. Salamon (ed.), *The State of Nonprofit America* (Washington, D.C.: Brookings Institution, 2002).

12. For an overview of how to cope with overwhelming situations, see R. Carlson, *Don't Sweat the Small Stuff—and It's All Small Stuff* (New York: Hyperion, 1997). The book deals with the stresses individuals experience dealing with complex situations like crises. Our focus is on relieving stress on the organizational level and how managers, as stressed out as they might be, can take action successfully.

13. The recent work of I. Mitroff focuses on corporate crises and ways to respond rather than react. A good introduction can be found in I. I. Mitroff and G. Anagnos, *Managing Crises Before They Happen:*

What Every Executive Needs to Know About Crisis Management (New York: AMACOM, 2000).

14. For an introduction to how cultural norms and values are reflected in managerial decision making, see K. A. Jehn and K. Weigelt, "Reflective Versus Expedient Decision Making: Views from East and West" in S. J. Hock, H. C. Kunreuther, and R. E. Gunther (eds.), *Wharton on Making Decisions* (Hoboken, N.J.: Wiley, 2001).

Chapter Two

1. Many of the efforts to make government bureaucracy more efficient and effective in the 1990s were based on business principles. D. Osborne and T. Gaebler's *Reinventing Government: How the Entrepreneurial Spirit Is Transforming the Public Sector* (New York: Plume, 1993) is a good introduction to the issues related to transferring commercial models to the public sector.

2. See P. F. Drucker, "What Businesses Can Learn from Nonprofits," *Harvard Business Review,* 1989, *67,* 88–93.

3. The Center for Social Innovation at Stanford University's Graduate School of Business has been a leader in transferring knowledge from the commercial sector to facilitate nonprofit change and improvement. Much of its work has focused on venture philanthropy models. For an overview of the center and its research, programs, and publications, consult its Web site: www.gsb.stanford.edu/csi/.

4. The comprehensive framework for the investment due diligence process can be found in J. J. Camp, *Venture Capital Due Diligence: A Guide to Making Smart Investment Choices and Increasing Your Portfolio Returns* (Hoboken, N.J.: Wiley, 2002).

5. A simple legal definition of *due diligence* can be found in B. A. Garner (ed.), *Black's Law Dictionary, Abridged,* 8th ed. (St. Paul: Thomson/West, 2005). It means "the diligence reasonably expected from a person who seeks to satisfy a legal requirement or to discharge an obligation" (p. 382).

6. A detailed overview of the due diligence process for mergers and acquisitions can be found in A. R. Lajoux and C. M. Elson, *The Art of M&A Due Diligence* (New York: McGraw-Hill, 2000). The due diligence process in developing business partnerships is addressed in S. Gerdes, *Navigating the Partnership Maze: Creating Alliances That Work* (New York: McGraw-Hill, 2002).

Chapter Three

1. A practical introduction to the issues related to group decision making can be found in S. Kaner and others, *The Facilitator's Guide to Participatory Decision-Making* (Gabriola Island, B.C.: New Society Publishers/Canada, 2002).

2. Many models of rational choice address the development and selection of alternative courses of action. For a solid and accessible overview of how choices are generated and selected, see Chapter Two in E. F. Harrison, *The Managerial Decision-Making Process*, 3rd ed. (Boston: Houghton Mifflin, 1995).

Chapter Four

1. Also referred to as a Pugh matrix, this method for decision support was initially developed by Stuart Pugh at the University of Strathclyde in Glasgow, Scotland, in the 1980s. See S. Pugh, *Total Design: Integrated Methods for Successful Product Engineering* (Reading, Mass.: Addison-Wesley, 1991).

2. See Committee on Theoretical Foundations for Decision Making in Engineering Design, National Research Council, *Theoretical Foundations for Decision Making in Engineering Design* (Washington, D.C.: National Academies Press, 2001).

3. See R. Fernandez, *Total Quality in Purchasing and Supplier Management* (Boca Raton, Fla.: CRC Press, 1997).

4. See G. Brue, *Design for Six Sigma* (New York: McGraw-Hill, 2003).

FURTHER READING

Camp, J. J. *Venture Capital Due Diligence: A Guide to Making Smart Investment Choices and Increasing Your Portfolio Returns.* Hoboken, N.J.: Wiley, 2002.

Drucker, P., and others. *Harvard Business Review on Decision Making.* Boston: Harvard Business School Press, 2001.

Fischer, M. *Ethical Decision Making in Fund Raising.* Hoboken, N.J.: Wiley, 2000.

Harrison, E. F. *The Managerial Decision-Making Process.* (3rd ed.) Boston: Houghton Mifflin, 1995.

Hoch, S. J., Kunreuther, H. C., and Gunther, R. E. (eds.) *Wharton on Making Decisions.* Hoboken N.J.: Wiley, 2001.

Kaner, S., and others. *The Facilitator's Guide to Participatory Decision-Making.* Gabriola Island, B.C.: New Society Publishers Canada, 2002.

March, J. G. *Primer on Decision Making: How Decisions Happen.* New York: Free Press, 1994.

Nutt, P. C. *Making Tough Decisions: Tactics for Improving Managerial Decision Making.* San Francisco: Jossey-Bass, 1989.

Weick, K. E., and Sutcliffe, K. M. *Managing the Unexpected: Assuring High Performance in an Age of Complexity.* San Francisco: Jossey-Bass, 2001.

Yates, J. F. *Decision Management: How to Assure Better Decisions in Your Company.* San Francisco: Jossey-Bass, 2003.

Young, D. (ed.). *Effective Economic Decision-Making by Nonprofit Organizations.* New York: Foundation Center, 2002.

INDEX